Sacred

Cows . . .

and Other   DISCARD

Edibles

ALSO BY NIKKI GIOVANNI

Vacation Time
Cotton Candy on a Rainy Day
The Women and the Men
Black Feeling, Black Talk/Black Judgement
Re: Creation
Spin a Soft Black Song
Gemini
A Dialogue: James Baldwin and Nikki Giovanni
My House
*A Poetic Equation: Conversations Between
Nikki Giovanni and Margaret Walker*
Ego Tripping and Other Poems for Young Readers
Those Who Ride the Night Winds

SACRED COWS . . . AND OTHER EDIBLES

NIKKI GIOVANNI

QUILL/WILLIAM MORROW/NEW YORK

Some of these articles have appeared in: *The Boston Globe; Essence* magazine; *Black Women Writers, 1950–1980,* edited by Mari Evans; *The Crusader* (Cincinnati), *USA Today,* and *Touchstone* magazine.

It is the policy of William Morrow and Company, Inc., and its imprints and affiliates, recognizing the importance of preserving what has been written, to print the books we publish on acid-free paper, and we exert our best efforts to that end.

Library of Congress Cataloging-in-Publication Data

Giovanni, Nikki.
  Sacred cows—and other edibles/Nikki Giovanni.
  p.   cm.
  ISBN 0-688-08909-7
  I. Title.
PS3557.I55S24   1989
814'.54—dc19

89-30979
CIP

Printed in the United States of America

First Quill Edition

  3   4   5   6   7   8   9   10

BOOK DESIGN BY MANUELA PAUL

◆ ◆ ◆ ◆ ◆ ◆ ◆ ◆

For Lillian, DST,
and
Jackie, AKA
my friends, who will
always be with me

◆ ◆ ◆ ◆ ◆ ◆ ◆ ◆

Contents

◆ ◆ ◆ ◆ ◆ ◆ ◆ ◆ ◆ ◆ ◆ ◆

ON SPAM,
USED CARS
AND MORE
OF THE SAME

◆ ◆ ◆ ◆ ◆ ◆ ◆ ◆ ◆ ◆ ◆ ◆

ON SPAM, USED CARS AND MORE OF THE SAME

I just went out and bought myself a pair of designer jeans —two pairs actually—and two designer T-shirts to go with them. Sure, I know I can't afford them, but being Black carries a special responsibility in this recession. I got a new car too. "What the heck," said I. Folks in Detroit could start pulling in their belts on poetry if they just wanted to be practical; then where would we be? It's not easy to be a proper consumer. People like to think, "Oh, anybody can spend money," but it's not true. Non-Blacks tend to ask the rate of return, the longevity of the product, its tax deductibility. Blacks, for the most part, make economic decisions on the first law of capitalism: "I Want It."

Look at what happened to the housing industry the minute we finally said we wouldn't have a home in the suburbs if they changed the stop lights to red, black and green. Construction fell off— that's what happened. Look at automobiles for that matter. They laughed and laughed at us and our big cars. We finally said, "Fine. Chrysler can take a New Yorker and do what is physically impossible with it." Of course with the General Electric sponsorship of Reagan we turned to Japanese electronics. The yen is solid; the dollar continues to fail.

I really think America should strike a special medal for the veterans of the sixties. This country, unique among the industrialized nations, has not experienced a war on its shores since 1865. What would our cities look like if Blacks hadn't had both the foresight and the courage to burn them down? Look at the money non-Blacks made with the commissions, studies, designs, constructions, reconstructions we made possible! For that matter, how many extra policemen were hired and drew overtime to contain us? How many social workers? Look at the button and poster industry in the sixties and compare that to 1982! All those people gainfully employed on Black Power buttons (with a panther in the corner), and MAKE LOVE NOT WAR posters, are now filling our welfare rolls. Take a peek at publishing. All those books to explain Blacks to Negroes and other non-Blacks. We, in fact, made California wines since liberals had to have parties for us and didn't want to serve their good German whites or French reds (and knew very well not to even chill their Portuguese rosés)! Doctors—and dare I mention them . . . lawyers! So many people were physically and mentally hurt, their numbers have more than doubled and their salaries quadrupled. A medal is not nearly enough. Guaranteed income is more like it.

If white Americans think about it they owe us a lot. We kept the Constitution alive by constantly testing it. We kept the country mentally united through the fear of The Riot. (When will It show up in your neighborhood?) Did they think it was easy? Fun? No! It was our sacrifice to the belief that They were better people than they thought they were. It was our own contribution to compassion. Since we have been afraid for two hundred years we helped them be afraid for a decade and we thought some good, some communication would come of shared concerns. But they seem determined to show us that once again we are wrong. They want to prove they are petty, ignorant and indifferent to the human condition. I must say this to my fellow and sister Americans who are not Black: Blacks hate a white person with no class. You sometimes think the kids on the street who are menacing you hold your color against you. No. It's the lack of class this nation is showing. It's the stupidity of always picking the wrong team to cheer for. It's the smallness of telling the young and old, the poor and dispossessed to go take a flying you-know-what. I mean, you just can't have your drunken daddy working on WPA and hate the poor. That is no style at all.

But the question is: Is it too late for America to regain Black confidence? Do we really care to sacrifice for these people again? I'm still doing my part. Not only do I use my Visa, which keeps the merchants busy; I have to be billed each month; I have to be called several times by one woman; I get a letter from someone else reminding me that I have not paid; I get a phone call from another man. That's five people right there who are working solely because of me. Lord knows I'm trying. But then, I appreciate and understand the level of sacrifice. When the rest of the country understands that money ought to be in the hands of people like me who have the faith, the courage, the willingness to spend even when we don't need and can't afford, then this recession will ease, the economy will turn up and Blacks, the consummate consumers, will regain our rightful place at the table of plenty. Otherwise, it's Spam, used cars and more of the same.

THE CINCINNATI SERIES

♦ ♦ ♦ ♦ ♦ ♦ ♦ ♦ ♦ ♦ ♦ ♦ ♦

ON HANDICAPS, SEAT BELTS, RISKS AND REASON

PART I

Recently, a friend of mine, through no lack of sensitivity, on a rainy day in Florida, pulled into a handicapped parking place. Well, the parking space wasn't handicapped, it was simply so designated. She's hardly the kind of person who would lie to a blind vendor, passing a one-dollar bill off as a five; she'd never, ever, under any circumstances take pencils from the street vendor and not pay. Hey! I've known her all my life; she's well bred. She, when she was without automobile, rode the public buses and always gave her seat to the elderly, disabled and pregnant. I've never known her to push ahead at the supermarket when an older patron has left a gap in the line. She has a teenage daughter whom she is rearing, which in and of itself should be a ticket to heaven. She uses her lunch hour to take her daughter to work, meaning no food, no rest, no break. She picks up her daughter at 11:00 P.M., meaning no kick back with a beer after work, no letup. She's uncomplaining. Yet she got a hundred-dollar ticket for parking in a handicapped place. Somehow it seems so unfair. If a Black woman rearing a teenager alone isn't handicapped, then I don't know who is. She didn't roost in the spot, she parked: prudently turned off her motor, took her keys, ran in, picked up her paycheck and came out to a one-hundred dollar ticket. I've never seen the physically impaired ticketed for parking in a spot designated for the temporarily able-bodied. I'm not necessarily against being sensitive to the needs of others, but I shop at the new Krogers several times a week since I have recently become quite inefficient and have yet to see eight handicapped shoppers' cars parked in the designated spots. I toyed with the idea of having a sticker made of my day. You know, just little time blocks: 5:30 A.M. me letting my dogs out/ 5:45 A.M. me wiping up the floor after Wendy, who is fourteen and incontinent/ 6:00 A.M. me calling teenage son, starting breakfast, letting dogs back in, getting morning paper, starting load of laundry in washer, trying to pour cup of coffee, struggling to keep eyes open, heart warm, manner calm. I think my mornings qualify for something. Is there no compassion for the ordinary?

I noted recently Gay Power is asserting itself for a special school for young gays in New York City. In Louisville a white worker was granted workmen's compensation because it made him nervous to work with Blacks. I guess we can look forward to the city council single-handedly taking the entire board of the Ohio Public Employees Retirement Fund hostage until they change their stock portfolio! Life seems so unfair lately to those of us who are ordinary. Ordinary people who saved their money in places like Home State so that they could take a trip to Greece end up being hijacked by people they never heard of for a cause they hold no feelings for or against. I mean, whatever happened to fair play?

But hey. We were discussing designated handicapped parking. At the risk of sounding a bit cold—if they can drive, they can take their chances along with the rest of us. Or I'm going to ask James Meredith to initiate a march demanding designated COLORED parking spots. Then, of course, the militant gays will demand designated gay spots, though everyone who laughs may lay a claim to those places, then white people will want designated white spots, then child abusers, then abused children, and dammit, there won't be any spots in town where normal cars can park, which is what it's all about anyway.

Otherwise we may as well dust off the old Black laws of a hundred years ago and begin the new loving, sensitive segregation instead of, I suppose, the old mean, evil kind. There must be a difference, but right now it's the forest and the trees to me.

PART II

Don't get me wrong. My interest in dying is right up there with my desire to see Beirut, save with Home State or have Reagan's new tax package passed. Excuse me. Reagan doesn't have a new tax package, he offers us a Revenue Enhancing Plan that will actually save people like me thousands and thousands of dollars. That one for sure is sitting on the desks of folks who say Divest Now and and earn millions or join the people who win at the New Ohio State Lottery. Naw, I'm being unfair. The New Ohio State Lottery gives you some chance, if not of winning at least of being happy you played, which is more than can be said of the others. But that has nothing to do with our topic of the day.

You see, I'm from Lincoln Heights, a small community about fifteen miles north of Cincinnati, directly across the expressway from General Electric. If the Feds hadn't built I-75, Lincoln Heights could make a good case for owning the land upon which GE was built. I mean, if Kentucky could sue Ohio over ownership of the Ohio River we could probably *win* our case. Those of us who are paranoid see the expressway as a part of the continuing policy to deprive those of us who settled the valley of our rightful wealth. Though, in the spirit of fairness, I should also acknowledge the tales of mayors who sold Lincoln Heights out. We in Lincoln Heights, lest we stray too far, are a rugged individualist community. We believe in doing it for ourselves.

You see, I think the new seat belt policy rates right up there with the missionary position. Something you do if your mate insists, something you may in fact have reason to want to do sometimes, but never the sort of thing that's designated by law. Even, and this pushes me, even if the insurance companies said, "Well, OK, if you have an accident and your seat belt was not on and you are hurt, your deductible will go up," I could maybe see it. It's still coercion, but it's a gentle coercion that allows me to feel I have some choice in the matter. I have heard testimony from friends and total strangers who swear by their belts. I'm glad. I want all who like being strapped in to swear by it. But it's funny, isn't it, if *Hustler* magazine ran a cover with a grown woman strapped in a car with a policeman standing over her saying, "Good girl," every born-again would howl. Now, yes, I know, someone will say, "Hey as much as you fly, how can you take that position . . . er, ump . . . stand?" I put my seat belt on in an airplane because it obviously makes the pilot feel so much better. Do you honestly think that I or any other passenger believes, as we roar off at approximately 500 mph, if we have to abort those little jokers won't cut us in half? We know damned well they will, which is why we pray, chant or distract ourselves with thoughts of the coming meal. If you think I or any passenger believes we will survive a plunge from forty thousand feet to planet Earth because we are strapped, you also think Close-Up will get you a boyfriend, Downy will make your kid write you from summer camp, and eating fiber will protect you from cancer. Hey, I know. I see the letters coming in right now: "I've been eating fiber for forty years and am still cancer-free." I'm glad. I want the world to be happy, healthy and sane. But somehow, I also want to get into my car, pop a cassette into place and drive off. If I speed, please stop me; if I'm drunk, please get me off the road and into jail; if I fail to stop at a stop sign, please ticket me; if I cause an accident or hurt someone, please, please charge me, but don't make me wear a seat belt by law. When I strap in, it ought to be by my own choice, or my desire to please my pilot.

◆ ◆ ◆ ◆ ◆ ◆ ◆ ◆ ◆ ◆ ◆ ◆ ◆ ◆

CITIZEN RESPONSIBILITY

(Hey! I'm Running for Office!)

I'm thinking about running for Cincinnati City Council. "Idiot," I hear out there, "you can't run for Council. You don't even live in the city!" Well neither does Sy Murray's secretary; neither will the new chief of police. Hey, lots of folks probably don't even live in Ohio who are working on the Cincinnati Convention Annex! Some folks, I'll bet, aren't even citizens who play on our baseball team. Why not a representative from Lincoln Heights? You'd get a fresh perspective from an ordinary person for a change.

OK, so I know someone is saying, but hey, what about Reading—Norwood—Woodlawn—Winton Terrace, for Christ's sake? It's not the same, that's why. Only Lincoln Heights and Cincinnati have a council where most members feel they are gods. Lincoln Heights and Cincinnati both have had to make drastic cuts to cover up for past foolishness. Neither area has adequate police and fire protection. That alone gives me a leg up. Plus I'm fun.

My platform?

1. Annex northern Kentucky. All the way to the Florence Mall.

It would stop all the petty criminal activity of purchasing liquor and cigarettes from another state. Newport and Covington are as nice as any other suburb on this side of the river, and it could smooth the transition for Appalachians making their way to the big city.

2. Annex Hamilton County. Let's face it: If Cincinnati gets a cold the county sneezes. Annexation will stop all the discussions about who lives where, not to mention overlapping taxes and underlapping services.

3. Annex Kings Island and the Jack Nicklaus Sports Complex. Sure Butler County will be upset, but so are the residents of Over-the-Rhine, and who listens to them?

4. Turn Union Terminal back into a transportation terminal. Greyhound and Trailways would move into the terminal. Keep it open twenty-four hours a day. Sure we'd need security, and by God that's a fine point. People can get work again. Use it for a bus pickup and drop-off for the airport. Keep the cab lines at the terminal and reduce the clutter downtown. People will need food and drinks while they're waiting. Hey, it could be a bonanza!

5. Consider public school teachers and all our librarians public servants of the highest order. Give them exactly twice the pay and all the benefits of police and fire people. Sure ... sure, it'll cost in the short run, but in the long run we just might come up with a civilized populace. Run school twenty-four hours a day, eliminating that I-don't-have-time-to-attend excuse. Make ignorance a choice, not an excuse or defense.

My pledge to the voters: I will look out, to the best of my ability, for the good of the citizens of Cincinnati even at the expense of not making dumb headlines and occasionally at the risk of doing nothing. Sure I'm being a little hard-nosed, but hey, these are hard times! NIKKI—INFLEXIBLE AND UNFAIR has a certain ring to it, don't you think? NIKKI—A MADE-UP MIND IS A TERRIBLE THING TO WASTE. Now that's a class bumper sticker. I mean, what more honorable a pursuit for an aging poet than to serve the city that nurtured her? NIKKI—WHY NOT THE ORDINARY?

♦ ♦ ♦ ♦ ♦ ♦ ♦ ♦ ♦ ♦ ♦ ♦ ♦

ON HOLIDAYS
AND HOW TO
MAKE THEM WORK

A proper holiday, coming from the medieval "holy day," is supposed to be a time of reflection on great men, great deeds, great people. Things like that. Somehow in America this didn't quite catch on. Take Labor Day. On Labor Day you take the day off, then go to the Labor Day sales and spend your devalued money with a clerk who is working. And organized labor doesn't understand why it suffers declining membership? Pshaw. Who wants to join an organization that makes you work on the day it designates as a day off? Plus, no matter how hidden the agenda, who wants a day off if they make you march in a parade and listen to some politicians talk on and on about nothing.

Hey. I'm a laborer. I used to work in Walgreen's on Linn Street. We were open every holiday and I, being among the junior people, always "got" to work the time-and-a-half holidays. I hated those people who came in. Every fool in the Western world, and probably in this universe, knows that Christmas is December 25. Has been that way for over a thousand years, yet there they'd be, standing outside the door, cold, bleary-eyed, waiting for us to open so they could purchase a present. Memorial Day, which used to be Armistice Day until we got into this situation of continuous war, was the official start of summer. We would want to be out with our boyfriends barbecuing . . . or something, but there we were behind the counter waiting to see who forgot that in order to barbecue you need: (1) a grill, (2) charcoal, (3) charcoal starter. My heart goes out to the twenty-four-hour grocery people, who are probably selling meat!

But hey. It's the American way. The big Fourth of July sales probably reduced the number of fatal injuries as people spent the entire day sober in malls, fighting over markdowns. Minor cuts and bruises were way up, though, I'll bet. And forget the great nonholiday, Presidents' Day. The damned thing could at least have a real name. What does that mean—Presidents' Day? Mostly that we don't care enough to take the time to say to Washington and Lincoln: Well done. But for sure, as a Black American I've got to go for it. Martin Luther King, Jr.'s birthday has come up for the first time as a national holiday. If we are serious about celebrating it, Steinberg's will be our first indication: GHETTO BLASTERS 30% OFF! FREE TAPE OF "I HAVE A DREAM" WITH EVERY VCR PURCHASED AT THE ALL-NEW GIGANTIC MARTY'S BIRTHDAY SALE. Then Wendy's will, just maybe, for Black patrons (and their liberal sympathizers) Burn-A-Burger to celebrate the special day. Procter & Gamble will withhold Clorox for the day, respectfully requesting that those Black spots be examined for their liberating influence. But what we really want, where we can know we have succeeded, is that every Federated department store offers 50 percent off to every colored patron who can prove he or she is Black in recognition of the days when colored citizens who were Black were not accorded all the privileges of other shoppers. That will be a big help because everybody will want to be Black for a Day. Sun tanneries will make fortunes during the week preceding MLK Day. Wig salons will reap great benefits. Dentists will have to hire extra help to put that distinctive gap between the middle front teeth. MLK Day will be accepted. And isn't that the heart of the American dream?

I really love a good holiday—it takes the people off the streets and puts them safely in the shopping malls. Now think about it. Aren't you proud to be with Uncle Sam?

REFLECTIONS ON
MY PROFESSION

♦ ♦ ♦ ♦ ♦ ♦ ♦ ♦ ♦ ♦ ♦ ♦ ♦

IN SYMPATHY
WITH ANOTHER
MOTHERLESS CHILD
(One View of the Profession of Writing)

Writing is like any other profession—breakdancing, ninth grade, doctor of philosophy, surgeon—it's what I do to justify the air I breathe, the food I ingest, the time I take up on earth. I'm ever and still amazed that any artist considers himself God or in close proximity thereof. It's not like a double 0 number—it's not a license to kill, no excuse to not exercise normal courtesy in human relations, no copyright to bigotry. I suppose there is, or at least there appears to be, some human need to cull from the general stock those who should be exalted. I don't trust that instinct at all. The more you are in public life, the less likely it is that your life will be worth living, unless you exercise great care to be sure it's your life and not what someone wants your life to be that you are living. I feel as sorry for the modern politicians and rock stars as I do the Roman Claudius, who was told by his Praetorian guards that he had one of two choices: "You will be emperor or we will kill you." Ass-kissing is not a normal human posture for the kisser or the kissee.

I am not at all sure that forty is the proper age to look at a career. At forty, first of all, the body changes. No one in his right mind would ask a teenager to write or evaluate his life, because those who have been through adolescence know that every day there is another major change, another crisis, another reason to feel life sucks and there is nothing that can be done about it. I'm not sure that at forty we know much more. At sixteen we can feel there will be another sixteen and another and another; at forty you pretty well know there will not be another forty; you are pleased to think there might be another ten, and depending upon the rate of body deterioration you can hope for another twenty with the coda: If I'm healthy. Most Americans are medically indigent; I know I am. I have instructed my mother to sign nothing should I be struck with any disease more serious than cellulite. I'm probably going to die anyway and there's no point in her, my son and my dogs going into bankruptcy to stave off the inevitable. Can we talk? It's not at all that I'm interested in dying. As a matter of fact I think life is one of the more interesting propositions offered on earth; it's just that I have lived through a terminal illness and have seen.

I like my profession. I hope the telephone operators, the hamburger turner at McDonald's, the pressure checker at Kentucky Fried who sees to it that those spices and herbs get really deep in the chicken are proud, too. I know some degree of incentive is necessary to my profession. Writers are the world's biggest procrastinators and the second biggest paranoid group, being bested only by politicians. I know that we have to get some kind of seed in our craw to write, and then we only write after we have washed all the windows, cleaned the oven, weeded the garden and are threatened with either bodily harm by our publishers or imminent bankruptcy by our creditors. I have a dear friend who invites me each summer to come to her home to write. "You'll have lots of privacy," she always points out, "and there are the swimming pool and the tennis courts when you need to take a break." What she has also figured out is that her closets will be both straightened out and waxed, her silver will get polished, all repairs will be made on the porch furniture, all doorknobs will be tightened. I'm very handy. In fact, I'm a joy to have around! I paint, stain, rescreen, file crystal; the only thing I don't do well in a house is electrical work that requires the box to be turned off. I'm terribly handy with plumbing and have been known in my mother's house to repair roof shingles. Of course, we seldom mention that the books don't get written . . . To tell the truth, my secret desire is to open my own Nikki's Best Handy Girl Service. Hey! If this poetry doesn't work out, I've got my second career all planned. As you may have guessed—I'm compulsive.

Ecclesiastes teaches us there is a season and a purpose for everything under the heavens; what it fails to mention is there is a place. I really can stand dirt since in my mind there is a purpose for dirt; I cannot stand disorder. I am stupefied, amazed, that people haven't alphabetized their books and records, that clothes in the closet don't hang on proper hangers in color and length categories. An unbalanced closet is the sign of a sick mind, much more indicative of the true personality than a cluttered desk, for which there is at least one excuse. It used to be that you could tell all you needed to know about a woman by the way she kept house; the same is true of men these days. Chalk one up for the ERA.

Rage is to writers what water is to fish. A laid-back writer is like an orgasmic prostitute—an anomaly—something that doesn't quite fit. I have been considered a writer who writes from rage, and it confuses me. What else do writers write from? We are not, after all, songsters who put together a ditty because the bride is not a virgin and the groom is impotent. Can't you see the new Broadway musical—*Come Together* (a musical experience based on the songs of John Lennon and Paul McCartney with five—count them— new songs!) As their mutually exclusive problems come to light on their wedding night, this scene unfolds:

HE: [*Stage right in a bolero-cut smoking jacket and red bikini underwear. The orchestra strings hit high C*] Ohhhh—I'd love to be able to screw you . . . [*in That falsetto country tenor he's so noted for*]

SHE: [*On the bed center stage, butt naked, though the audience can't tell because her long tresses are covering her*] I need your dick tonight . . .

HE: [*Flicking his braids and rising to tiptoe over the bed*] But since I can't pursue you . . .

SHE: [*With that famous lip pout, pointing her toes in that gymnastic move so popular last year on the Sri Lanka tour*] And we can't get it right . . .

BOTH: [*She rises from the bed; he moves stage left and offers his right hand, giving full view to the audience*] Let's get funky, funky, funky . . . [*They break out in a series of twirls*] Let's just screw the best we can . . . [*Both kick leg high in opposite directions*] Let's get funky, funky, funky . . . till we don't give a damn . . .

Of course "Funky, Funky, Funky" goes on to be the number one hit on the Pop charts and number three on Soul (according to *Variety*). "The Original Cast Come Together" stays at number one for thirty-two weeks in a row, setting a new record for Broadway musical albums. Forget that it says nothing and doesn't even rhyme; the writer, Dave "Mr. Rock Steady" Cummings, is on all the TV talk shows, and the artistic world hails his shocking innovations. It did more than add to his body of human knowledge, it did something more important than helping people grow and understand their problems—it did the most important thing a song can do . . . it sold!

A poet couldn't get away with that. Sure, I know Bob Dylan, as well as Lennon-McCartney, are considered poets, but that's only because we want to pay them a compliment. If Francis Scott Key and the man who wrote "Trees" hadn't had their poems set to music, no one would even think to listen to them today. I mean Dr. J. is poetry in motion, too, but we don't put that in stanzas. And as weird as Dylan has become lately, he hasn't become that weird. Why, someone would cart him off the stage into the nearest state-run mental hospital, because if he's that gone why waste the money? "I will now read from my song . . ." No. A poet has to say something. A poem has to make some sort of sense; be lyrical;

to the point; and still be able to be read by whatever reader is kind enough to pick up the book. Certainly there are poets who deliberately use language to obscure the fact that they have nothing to either share or convey, but we aren't discussing them. Those would be the academicians who write for each other and, let us not forget, to impress the department head. I have even gone so far as to think one of the duties of this profession is to be topical, to try to say something about the times in which we are living and how we both view and evaluate them. Relevance will lead to either critical ridicule or total dismissal. One of the most severe criticisms of Rod McKuen is that people read and enjoy him. Imagine! What nerve! Poetry isn't to be read and enjoyed. It's to be difficult, dark, full of hidden meanings, allegorical, with strange images in even stranger words about some other poet no one ever heard of. If Black writers write about slavery, we are told it's parochial, no one is interested in this stuff; but when Jewish writers write about their history it's called the Old Testament. When women write about the reality of our lives, it's called too dull; when white men write their lives, it's called heroic. The ultimate literary confrontation will be the Old Testament Meets the New Holocaust vs. Deliverance of the Man in the Gray Flannel Suit. You the reader are invited to compare these two marvelous anthologies by some of our greatest writers. You can use the coupon at the bottom of this page to check your preference for the work of the millennium, and while you're at it we're sure you will want to buy these two black glove-leather–bound copies for your children. For only $5.95 down and $5.00 a week for the next 250 weeks we will put these right on your bookshelf. And if you order now and mention Joe sent you we will give you free of charge this marvelous bookmark blessed by three living rabbis and two popes. Don't miss This opportunity to help hubby get ahead and the kiddies do better in school. Phooey!

I think a lot of the Black poets because we honor the tradition of the grioes. We have traveled the length and breadth of the planet singing our song of the news of the day, trying to bring people closer to the truth. As the written word became both possible and accessible, poets such as Dante, Milton, and T. S. Eliot carried on the African tradition. Though some people were as unhappy with our "motherfuckers" as in other times some were shocked by Chaucer's eroticism, some people were simply born to be shocked.

On a scale of 1 to 10 I have to admit literary excess is about 380. Whether it's done smoothly or crudely; whether it's the ravings of *Mein Kampf* or American Unionists in 1852 clutching *Uncle Tom's Cabin*. It's neither *The Klansman* nor *The Strawberry Statement* that causes action; it is action that gives life to literature. I do confess to being shocked. I am not, nor do I recommend a state of, blasé that accepts any and everything. But what is shocking to me will never come from the lips of Prince on a record but rather from the lips of the New Bedford men *for* the record who. stated she must have really wanted to be raped on a pool table or else why would she have needed a pack of cigarettes after the 7-Eleven closed?

I am totally shocked by the Cincinnati father who raped his five-month-old baby while his wife was out shopping. Guess that will teach his wife to ask him to baby-sit. I'm shocked that child molesters now simply open day care centers to which unwitting parents take innocent children. I'm shocked that people, estimated in the millions, will die of starvation on this earth; that people sleep in the crevices and corners of the streets in our major cities; that mass murderers and attempted presidential assassins get to plead mental anguish. Talk about a headache! I'm disappointed that Ronald Reagan thinks trees pollute and that the Democratic party nominated Walter Mondale. But hey! Who asked me? I'm sorry that every time I like a television program it goes off the air. That kind of thing makes you feel like you are a one-woman Neilsen ("What does Giovanni like this season? Well, get it off!")

How we as a world got into book censorship is well beyond my powers to understand. It's really funny in a way. We can get *Little Black Sambo* off library shelves because Black Americans may be offended and it isn't even about Black Americans, but we support *Penthouse* and *Hustler* because of First Amendment protections. I'm not shocked at pornography, but it's awful. And what makes it so awful isn't naked women in totally absurd positions, but rather that somebody needs to make someone else submissive. But I attended a colored college, so I may have missed something. Maybe some reader will be kind enough to explain it to me because all I see is a married man angry because his mistress was unfaithful. The Miss America pageant gathers together all the winners of the fifty Miss State contests. They come to Atlantic City, which used to be just a playground for the rich and others who liked saltwater taffy and maybe an occasional Monopoly freak. They have never in their fifty-six-year history picked a girl of sturdy character, high intelligence, fluid articulateness who was ugly. They have never picked a girl who declined to participate in the swimsuit contest. They always say talent is important, but if what I see on-screen is what they call talent, either I am crazy or they are deaf. But hey! I'm not going to intimate that perhaps the true talent contest takes place in another arena and that the inability to properly judge that contest is what really cost Bert Parks his position. No. I will stick to my question. What is the difference between Bob Guccione and the other old pimps who make up the Miss America pageant? What is the difference between how any of them are using women to earn their living? In every issue, in every contest, both, like the butcher, look for fresh meat. What continues to make men think they have a right, first dibs actually, on the bodies of women? I like Vanessa Williams. Nobody would even ask me to pose naked, nor pay for the photographs should I insist, though my doctor just informed me I am at my optimum weight and for a woman of my age in pretty good health. Oh, I'm sorry. We weren't discussing health, were we, but rather looks.

I think it must be awful to be beautiful. No matter what anyone says, I don't think people cheer for beautiful people; I think they are jealous. It's bad enough being intelligent or truly talented, but at least you can hide that a lot by just not talking. But beauty is a walking billboard to every bimbo who has eyes. More than being delighted that Williams was chosen Miss America, it made my day. She is cute and seemed to have a lot of moxie. And, let's face it, it was damned boring to have all those little miss blondies paraded before us all the time. It was time for a radical change, and the pageant had one of two choices: an ugly white girl or a beautiful Black one. They made the right choice. Of the two Black women in the running I was pulling for Vanessa because she had a glint in her eye. I love a risk-taker; I liked her existential approach. Though she appeared to be happy she didn't look as if her whole damned life depended upon being chosen. She was cool. As it turned out she is still the best choice because she's been a thoroughbred all the way. Until the mess with *Penthouse* no one had anything other than praise for the way she handled herself, and even when they all crumbled Williams faced the print press and the television cameras with style. She never backed down; plus, as much as people don't like to deal with it, it's her body. If she would stand on the stage for the judges of the contest, why wouldn't she have posed nude for her boss? She had no more an obligation to mention the photographs than they did to acknowledge she was their ticket to ride. But maybe there is something else that bothers me more than the shabby treatment panicking old men meted out to a young woman. They reminded you, didn't they, of Alexander Haig when Reagan was shot. All panic and no purpose. Call a press conference! Sweat like Nixon! "I'm in charge here!" Denounce Williams. Sort of Rumpelstiltskinish ("The witches have told you my name!"), flailing wildly about for an anchor ("It's all her fault!"). They were pitiful. What happened to that "grace under pressure" of which Hemingway spoke so well? What happened to "Let's give her a chance to explain"? No. They looked like the first Lite Beer camping trip when Rodney joins the party: It's the creature! Which was not Vanessa Williams, but their own veneer so neatly stripped. It's the mirror Bob Guccione held for them and they, like Dorian Gray, saw who they really are—old, gray-chested men with ten tons of gold around their necks from which hang fifty-six little skulls (fifty-five ivory, one ebony), their prissy little mouths sprouting prissy little platitudes while the Poli-Grip worked overtime. The pageant men and Guccione did what some would have thought impossible—they made a compassionate man of Hugh Hefner. They made a graceful, articulate, caring man of the granddaddy of them all. And let us not forget their first pronouncement after demanding the burning of Vanessa was that the second runner-up is busy with her own career and obligations so we will go to the third. In other words, "Let's get a real white woman in here. Louisa will save the day yet." In walks Little Miss Muffet, though, to save the spiders from the curds and whey.

I saw the photographs. I am one of those who rewarded Guccione as I had previously rewarded John Dean and Jeb Magruder. Tacky would be a good word for both occasions. Naïve would be another. Having also viewed the work of David Hamilton (*Sisters; Country Cousins*), I found it highly credible that pornography passes as art; that someone who thinks her looks are the entrée rather than the appetizer would easily be persuaded to expose herself. I simply won't buy the this-is-a-fantasy-of-hers bull. Chaipel didn't tippy-toe into his studio with his Kodak Instamatic and catch two girls off guard. These photographs are obviously posed. And, frankly, had they been properly cropped, wouldn't have been too bad. What's wrong with naked women, as opposed to naked men, is that women don't pretend shock at the sight of a photo of a penis; men are always upset that another man will see what he "treasures." It's time for men to grow up. Sex isn't dirty-dirty or nasty-nasty. It's time men quit using the anatomy of a female against her; it's overdue that men quit using the penis as a weapon. But the most disgusting statement on the Williams situation that I read was in *USA Today*'s Opinion, in which a 20-year-old Black woman from "Hopeless," Georgia, said Vanessa had "let the race down." Little chipmunk-cheeked Bryant Gumbel leered the same question on the *Today* show. Then, in his role as Mr. Compassion, he wanted to know, "When do the tears come?" A friend of mine said Vanessa should have said, "Nigger, please!"

There were too many people who wanted to pretend that the sight of that young woman without her clothes on had set the human race back to the Stone Age; the American people closer to nuclear confrontation with Russia; Black people back to head-scratching and "Yessir, boss." I mean, what did she really do other than mistakenly believe she could utilize her own self? While Little Miss Muffet Charles (was "Do Dah" her talent entry?) tells the world she has no secrets. That's admirable. One in every four girls and one in every ten boys have secrets by the age of twelve. Three out of four people have halitosis. Some have even known the heartbreak of psoriasis. I join with Marvin Gaye in a salute: Right on. There is no reason to think Miss Charles understood she was chosen only to make sure Vanessa was not shot down by some crazy American. She thought the pageant had made a mistake in overlooking her in the first place. There is no reason to think she would accept the pageant's offer not to disrupt her schedule. ("But I have to follow the white rabbit," said Alice.) There was certainly no reason to think she would simply decline to participate in the humiliation of Vanessa. Oh no. She was the understudy whose moment had arrived. I alone raised the value of Excedrin stock that week. It all gave me a headache.

Actually, I'm not in a rage frequently. For some reason, after all these years, meanness and stupidity still get to me. I work on it, honestly. I understand not everyone has had the advantages I have enjoyed of being able to both read and digest material and apply the lessons learned. I'm told by my young friends that ex-perience is much more important than books. Of course Ben Franklin had something to say about experience and fools, but even Franklin thought that a fool would learn by his experience. That has proven false in the modern world. Some people are simply unwilling to learn under any circumstances, which maybe, even then, wouldn't be so bad if they weren't so damned proud of it. Doesn't it just make your skin crawl to hear somebody spout off about what they don't do and how they're never going to do it? It makes you cheer against the human race. I'm sure to be a crotchety old lady, assuming I have not yet achieved that state, because things like refusing to eat oysters will drive me up a wall. Stick one of the damned things in your mouth; then you can say, "I don't care for oysters, though I have tried them." This argument does not apply to cocaine or other hallucinogenic drugs; the experience of other people will do just fine. Isn't that the purpose of people living and sharing? So that others will at least not make the same mistake, since we seldom are able to re-create the positive things in life.

I guess one of life's experiences that I have always wanted to avoid was bitterness. Yes, I know I wrote a poem on bitterness and I know that earlier in this career critics thought I was bitter, but I am not nor was I. Just sick and tired of the same song and dance. The bitter people are as bad as the drug people because they seem to descend to a place from which no light ever emerges. I had an experience with the Interracial Council on Children's Books that pushed my bitter button, though. There is a book, *Jake and Honeybunch Go to Heaven*, which is illustrated by Margo Zemach, a white woman. She had taken the old Black folktale and placed it in the thirties. Jake and his mule, Honeybunch, are killed by a train because the mule wouldn't move out of the way. Jake gets to heaven first and, in his attempt to adjust, runs into trouble. He picks up two left wings, he sees a jazz band, there is a big fish fry . . . all the usual things. He finally meets God, who is a Black man with a white beard who tells him he'll have to leave because of the disturbance he is causing. Jake just misses Honeybunch, who has finally arrived in heaven. If Jake was a disaster, Honeybunch is a blind man with a pistol. No one can control the mule, so God sends for Jake, who promises to both control his mule and do better himself. God gives Jake the specific job of putting the stars and moon out, so if you look at the night sky and there is only darkness, just know that Jake and Honeybunch are probably off fishing and forgot to do their work. A really rather harmless story that has been around, for anyone who knows her folklore, for ages. From the same place as the modern-day "People Get

Ready (there's a train a'coming)" to "Oh Pray My Wings Are Going to Fit Me Well."

There were literary complaints that God was both male and Black, though I had a difficult time picturing Jake being greeted by Sheena of the Jungle or Marilyn Monroe. Some said one of the illustrations, which showed a Black man sleeping in a Pullman, wasn't real, but neither is the idea of the L. C. Greenwood and Bert Jones exchanging letters. Some didn't like the food Jake saw being cooked and consumed. I just had a difficult time trying to see Jake enjoying lox on an onion bagel. Some didn't like the jazz band in heaven. Mostly what none of them liked was that a white woman illustrated a Black folktale. Why, they cried, couldn't a Black illustrator have done it? Because a Black illustrator didn't, that's why. It neither added to nor subtracted from the book that was before us to ask that kind of question.

Anyway, the council decided to wage holy war against Jake and began lining up its Black pawns. My mother took a message for me to call the council. I returned the call and was told that the Jake situation was racist and something should be said about it. Being familiar with the council, though not its tactics, I asked if they would send me the book. I recalled several years ago they had accused *Sounder* of being racist because the book was named after the dog and the characters weren't given names. Since I hadn't been offended by *Sounder* I was at least cautious.

The book arrived the next day. I read it and looked at it carefully. After dinner I read it again. Since my mother is a much better folklorist than I could hope to be and since she has a special interest in children's literature, I asked her to read it for me. I called a librarian at the Cincinnati Public Library and asked her for an opinion, which she was unable to give because she had not seen the book, though she did supply me with additional material. I read the additional material. Neither my heart nor my mind could find any racist intent in *Jake and Honeybunch*. I could see why some people might not want to purchase a copy for their children, but that's hardly the same as condemning the book. Many people

don't want to purchase *Slaughterhouse Five, Catcher in the Rye,*
all of my books, but that doesn't mean a full-scale literary war
should be raised. Books are self-censoring agents. First they have
to be written, then they have to be published, then they have to
find their way into the homes or hands of readers, then they still
have to go the extra mile of being interesting enough to be read.
I figure books have a hard enough time without the added pressure
of false information leaking out about them.

I sat down and wrote the council a letter that ended, "I do not
find *Jake and Honeybunch* racist," which was a simple statement
of what I thought about the book. I don't like *Charlie and the
Chocolate Factory* because I didn't like the way the "Oompa Lum-
pas" were characterized; I really thought William Styron's *Nat
Turner* was just a total waste, but Dahl and Styron probably don't
read me either. I would not be disappointed to find that is so; I
would be disappointed to find that they demand the removal of
my books from the shelves. I wrote the council a long letter ex-
plaining my reasoning since it was more than obvious that *Jake*
was going to get reamed by most writers. I thought it the honorable
thing to do.

When the council's newsletter came out that fall, responses to
Jake ranged from, "Yes, it is racist and should be removed from
the shelves" to "Yes, it is racist but should be left alone" except
for one response—mine. Maybe I wouldn't have burned so much
if the council had published my whole letter or at least given some
of my reasoning. Since I was the only voice who spoke up for *Jake*,
it seemed to me only fair that a fuller explanation was needed than
"On the other hand," which listed me as saying I did not find *Jake
and Honeybunch* racist. What was the great fear? That the reasoning would be so persuasive that all others would repent? No.
The great fear, I think, is that one Black writer decided to say
what she believed. This little soldier didn't join Nixon's army,
neither would I start banning books.

About ten years ago James Earl Jones starred in an Off Broadway
production of a one-man show on Paul Robeson. Friends of mine

and people who knew Robeson were very upset with the portrayal and decided to take out an ad or something in *The New York Times* to protest. A friend called me and asked if I would join them. He explained their point of view and I said, "Yes." I did say to him that if anyone asked if I had seen the production I would be forced to tell them I signed out of friendship. The ad ran and I *was* asked about it by CBS local. James Earl Jones then said in *The Times* the next day he was disappointed with me because he expected more of me. I was actually ashamed. I had not even thought about James Earl or his feelings. I had only thought that I was helping out a friend. I knew I never wanted to feel that way again in my life. Not like a fool, because I have been a fool enough to know that doesn't matter one way or the other, but insensitive. If you're going to hurt people's feelings, it should definitely be because of something you believe in. In that way that people are when they learn something I'm glad James Earl expressed disappointment, otherwise it would never have crossed my mind again, and though I don't think my friend was exactly using me, I also know I seek no concurring opinions of my own beliefs.

When I saw the newsletter I felt compelled to write the council to tell them I thought they abused my good offices. Their response was to send me a Xeroxed copy of another book they didn't like. As fate would have it, the *Jake* controversy started with the refusal of the Milwaukee librarians to purchase copies for general circulation. The *Jake* publisher had accused them of censorship; they retaliated with racism. It just goes to show how wars get started. I had a speaking engagement in Milwaukee that fall. At the postreception I had the pleasure of meeting one of the librarians. She asked me if I had seen the newsletter and I sort of went off on her. Then she said, "You know, I did additional research, and the book is basically sound." "Are you going to write the author to let her know?" "Oh no. I still don't like the book," she said. "But you do see that not liking the book isn't the same as saying the book is racist?" "Yes. Well, but it's probably best to let things alone." I have an unshakable affection for librarians. I'm sure, because she was a charming lady who probably meant no harm, that there was some unstated reason like, "My job would be at stake"; "Nobody was really hurt"; "The Devil made me do it." Aren't those the traditional excuses we seek? The lessons of Nuremberg have yet to be learned. But at least we are all trying. Each in her own way. I hope.

Mine, like most families of writers, lives in absolute terror that one day I shall tire of contemplating my own navel and turn to theirs. The most at risk in this situation are, of course, children because we, the writers, can sign a release for them, the minors. I look any day now for the family of Erma Bombeck to file a class-action suit and take away her tennis court. I'm luckier than Ms. Bombeck because I don't have any tangible assets. They can only hope that I will one day peck into a megaseller, then bingo! They can pounce. Of course, this will never happen because I'm a poet.

But then, there are advantages to having a poet in the family. I write marvelous little thank-you notes with just the right touch of both joy and humility at receiving a present. I do nifty invitations. And Ma Bell or, rather, the new AT&T Regionals, owe me one because I have raised the art of letter-writing to the point that very few people in my family will write—they generally just reach out and touch.

The only one who has successfully escaped my poetic intrusion is my girl dog, Wendy, though I did, of course, dedicate a book to her because I got tired of her bitching that she was left out. Dogs are funny. If you write about them they accuse you of exploitation. Look at the heartache Lassie and her family went through—always having to do a heroic number to keep the affection of her owners; look at poor Rin Tin Tin, galloping across the plains leading the cavalry . . . then having to listen to Black Beauty and the others complain that *he* gets all the glory. What's even worse is that sexism is ever present. Lassie was played by a male, though of course you can't get away with that with horses. So I have low-keyed it with Wendy. She's a really marvelous cairn terrier with a highly developed sense of self and duty. Truth is, she would give her life for me. She's a great watchdog and will let you know when anything is awry. Her desire to protect me got her into trouble in the house because she would always bark at my father when he got up to go to the bathroom in the middle of the night. He would curse her and say clearly, mostly I think for my benefit, "Damned crazy dog!" I naturally had to support Wendy so I would get up and pet her and say, "Good girl." My mother would by that time have stumbled out of her room to see what the commotion was, which always woke up Bruno, my boy dog, who then had to go out himself, which meant someone had to wait on him since he never, in rain nor snow nor dark of night, could just go out and pee; he always had to patrol the entire backyard. Tommy slept through it all, which was just as well as he usually had left his TV running and would have been reamed at two o'clock in the morning for the waste.

Bruno, by the way, is worthless. If I ever hit Lotto and get a big house and new car and buy a lot of nifty things people would want to steal, I'll have to find a new home for him. Nothing on earth should be as friendly as that dog. He sucks up to repairmen, telephone guys, the Orkin man, anyone who comes to the door, no matter how menacing or strange-looking. My mother, when we moved back home, at first said two dogs were too much, but every morning while she worked her crossword puzzle he'd climb over her feet to put his head in her lap. Bru has her convinced that he is actually of help with some of the words. My cousin Pat, who lives in California, has Bruno out each summer, and he's such a nerd that she reads fairy tales to him before he goes to bed. He ignores me completely. If I just need something little, like help with getting a twig out of the way, he will pretend to be busy. The only thing I do that really delights him is make ice cream but, as I always tell him, I'm on to his tricks. He and Tommy like to wait until they hear me go "Uumph! UUmph!" knowing those are the last couple of turns, then they both come bounding over. I always give the dasher to Wendy 'cause she'll stick with me through the whole thing—to hell with that sometimey dog and boy. Mommy says I ignore Bru but it's his own fault. I'm the one who bought him and his food; who takes him to be groomed; who sees to it he has his shots. And who does he suck up to? Everybody else.

Now, as far as children go, I have no special insight into teenagers, save this: The fourteen-year-old personality was invented to give ulcers to otherwise calm mothers; to cause normally tranquil, proud, loving parents to snarl, growl and threaten; the fourteen-year-old personality was created, in other words, to drive forty-year-old mothers to the nuthouse.

Everyone says babies are difficult; it's just not true. Changing diapers, wiping pabulum from chins, heating bottles in the middle of the night are a snap compared to picking up your own telephone that you pay for every month and never hearing a familiar voice, either friend or relative, but rather a barbarian girl or boy demanding, "Tom home!" I was at first annoyed by the question and then by the tone, but I've trained myself to respond only to the question asked: "Why, yes, he is. How kind of you to call and inquire. I must go now." I then hang up. The barbarian response next was, "Can I speak to Tom?" to which I replied, again, as sweetly as possible: "It appears you are quite capable. I hear you very well. I must go now." Finally they reached the desired question: "May I speak to Tom?" which, unfortunately, elicits "I'm sorry, dear, but Thomas may not use the telephone until his grades improve." I don't add "Or hell freezes over."

Whichever comes first. Hell will surely win.

Why, sister mothers, do children want to fail? Is it the new high? Is there some sexual charge experienced when our ninth-graders come home with report cards full of F's and I's? What sado-psychological satisfaction is gained by them watching our hearts leap from our breasts, our eyes involuntarily tearing over, our breaths coming in short, unnatural spurts? What kick do they get standing over us watching our lives pass before our eyes? All my friends have marvelous children who clean their rooms, excel in extracurricular activities, pass their classes, get honors and awards. I've even taken, and I don't mind admitting it, to avoiding certain parents of perfect children, though I have not been a competitive parent. When little Billy Bob joined the Boy Scouts, climbed a twelve-story building and rescued a blind, paraplegic unwed mother from raging flames I never said to my son: "How come you never do anything worthwhile?" No. I smiled at the parent, congratulated the child and dutifully went back to pinning Tom's socks for the laundry and picking up the comic books that are spread across the floor, making his room a hazzardous area. When little Sally Mae, in just the fifth grade, was invited to Athens to address the Senate in her fluent Greek on how stability could be obtained with Turkey, I said to her mother, my friend, "You must be very proud." I did not say to Tom, "Why is it that that little snotty-nose twerp is hailed the world over while you refuse to write a simple essay for English *in* English about the Alaskan cruise I had to mortgage the house to take you on?" I didn't even heap abuse when he replied, "Alaska wasn't so much." No. I calmly said, "Dear, I sincerely think you can improve this Incomplete by turning in your assignment." I am, however, about to be convinced that kindness, civil tone, and logic have no truck with teenagers. My son had a classmate last year who was spanked every time she brought home a B or less. Tom was appalled. "But dear," I pointed out, "look at your grades and look at hers. Surely I am the parent in the wrong." "Well," says Mister as he makes his way to the freezer to get a pizza and pop it in the oven, "she hates her mother and I love you." If this is love, folks . . .

My son, I do believe and have had demonstrated, has a lot of character. He has never lied to me. I'm told by friends with perfect children that that is because it's all the same to him. He doesn't lie because he knows I won't go off on him or stop him from doing anything he wants to do anyway. I like to think that's not true. I like to think he is truthful because (1) I *will* go crazy on him if he lies; but mostly because (2) somewhere inside that pickled four-teen-year-old mass that commonly is called a brain he has absorbed some of the values I've been trying by example to teach him. When I am hasty in my judgments or just plain wrong about something

I don't mind apologizing. When I don't know something I don't mind admitting ignorance. When I don't want him to go somewhere or do something for no particular reason other than I think it's not right for him, I explain, "Mother is making an arbitrary judgment that has no logic or reason. You are right to be angry about this. I would feel the same way if the tables were turned." It may not be any easier to take, but it's honest.

I've also seen Tom come through a situation that would be difficult for a stable adult. My father developed bladder cancer following a stroke, which is the reason we moved from New York back to Cincinnati. Those years could not have been easy, living with someone who was, in fact, dying. My father was brave in the face of his impending death and so was my son. Neither complained of the burden or the pain. The night my father died Tom, my mother and I were the only ones at home. My sister was coming in from San Francisco. My nephew from Seattle was not contacted until the day after. The hospital called that Gus had died. I had to go out to pick up his personal property and sign for the autopsy. Tom, who was then twelve, said, "I'll go with you." He went to the hospital, viewed the body, got his grandfather's walking cane, stayed while the other arrangements were made. That night he came into my room and curled up next to Wendy, my dog, and slept on the floor. The next morning we had to pick a casket. "I'll go with you," he said to my mother, my sister and me. He put his tie and jacket on and sat through the funeral arrangements. He stayed by my side as the family made calls, placed flower orders, took care of the kind of base-touching a funeral requires. For two days he looked after us as best he could. On the morning of the funeral he asked: "Mommy, when is Chris getting here?" Meaning, I think, that he had gone as far as he was capable. It was more than caring . . . it was character.

Last year we visited a boarding school of note in the East. He and I stayed three days and he loved it. My child would prep in the ninth grade. I, too, would have something to brag about over beer and barbecue. As the three of us, Tom, my mother and I, talked over our fall plans I started outlining how he could have his own MasterCard, how to check his bank balance, the numbers to call to reach me wherever I might be, the numbers for Grandmother. Tom looked up and said: "Wait a minute! Where *are* you going to be?" "I'll be out working to pay for your tuition. That's why I'm going over these plans with you." "Well, where will Grandmother be?" "She'll be here a lot but she may want to travel, visit her sisters or anything else she wants to do." "You mean I'm going off BY MYSELF?" Eyes getting larger. "Well, yes, Tom. That's what it means to prep. You go off to school by yourself." In that let's-get-this-straight manner he says: "You're not taking an apartment in Wallingford?" "No." "Well I sure didn't think you were kicking me out" with just a touch of the indignant in his voice.

He went to public school. And turned fourteen. Since I know the school system is one of the best in the country, since I know he has the ability, I can only blame it on fourteen. My grandmother, Louvenia Watson, used to baffle me when she said, "I'll be glad when you get off Fool's Hill." I never used to know what she meant. I certainly do now. He'll turn fifteen this year and I, who was supposed to turn forty-one, will turn 103. As they sing in the coffee commercial with all the winners sitting around smiling: Hold on tight to your dream . . . Actually, though, I am a very hip mother. I was into Prince and Michael Jackson before Thomas realized what he could be in life. Yeah, sure, you'd like a kid who could pronounce perfect and not "purrfect," but I think the way Michael says it is cute. I know "Thriller" is in the *Guinness Book of World Records*, but there will always be a special place in my heart for "Rock with You." I haven't quite adjusted to parachute pants, but I'm into ties and boots—what I call my Tina Turner look, though I have an Afro. We can't all do long hair. I tend to be a bit old-fashioned, and nothing, absolutely nothing, will get me totally out of my elephant bells. I mean, the big chill may have settled on the rest but I'm going forward. The sixties stood for something.

I shall always remember the joy on my grandmother's face when she came back from the mass meeting to tell me I *could* march and how proud she was. She and Grandpapa caught a cab to come see me. I actually figured I was on my way to meet my maker, but one must have a sense of social responsibility. When I enrolled in Fisk University the following fall one of the things I most looked forward to was sitting in. There was a sort of style to it. Assuming you weren't actually molested, it was cool. You sat on the stool and watched the white people panic. Dick Gregory has the best story. When he stopped at a diner the waitress said, "We don't serve niggers," to which Gregory replied, "I don't eat them." You always hoped someone would say something to you to let you be cool. Mostly you were scared. I was home alone the Sunday the little girls were bombed in Birmingham. I remember the news flash saying they were dead. And it was enough to make you want to kill. Like all southern youngsters I went to Sunday school in a big church with a basement that could have hidden anything. It seemed so damned unfair.

Our personal tragedy in Knoxville was the bombing of Clinton High School. It really made you wonder about the people we lived among. Racism is at best boring. When I was younger it was frightening. You always felt someone was trying to kill you. Or hurt your feelings. Now it's just tiresome. Who really wants to be bothered with it anymore? It's dull to hate, though I doubt that my generation will ever be able to graft new emotions to the scars. Emmett Till; Schwerner, Chaney and Goodman; Nina Simone said it best: "Mississippi Goddamn!" The summer of '64 was frightening. All else became a release and to many a relief. And when you look at Miami where the police are back to shooting Black boys down or L.A. or New York, and anyone unfortunate enough to be arrested is committing suicide in jail, you really have to wonder, when will we learn? It's just so unworthy and spirit-sapping.

I do think we have been deeply touched by the past decade. Even the little things. We couldn't, in Knoxville, go to the movie theaters downtown or to the amusement park. I do like movies, but to this day I won't go to any amusement park. Cincinnati was no better. Coney Island, the local southern Ohio place to play for white kids, had to be sued before Blacks would be admitted. It's boring. Gwen Brooks and I shared a reading in New Jersey a few years ago and in the Q and A someone asked about racism in America. Gwen gave an intelligent response; I said it was boring. At lunch Gwen said, "Boring?" Well, what else do you call it? It can't be a sickness 'cause the cure is known. It's not a condition 'cause the times they did a change. It doesn't make anybody happy. I mean, I never ran into a hater who said, "You know, this hating business is really good." "It makes my day to deny a job to some Black man or woman." "I really love flunking the Black kids I have to teach." Or, "Yesterday I dumped my Black neighbor's garbage on his lawn and I just want you people to know how pleased I am with myself." We used to laugh at the Klan, which liked to think it was the sheets that frightened us. Hell, it was the men in the sheets, and we knew that all along. One of the sure signs that Blacks and whites are coming closer together, which is not necessarily for the good of this earth, is Black people have begun sneaking around doing murder for no reason, committing real suicide as opposed to the overdrinking–bad driving–fight-picking way we used to and standing around making reasonable-sounding excuses for our failure to live up to what we ourselves know to be our emotional potential and moral obligation. But hey, what does this have to do with autobiography?

I took a test recently in one of the popular magazines. I, not surprisingly, find myself quite an attractive personality, though my test score indicated that people find me opinionated and perhaps pushy. Not bad traits for writers. I know this profession does not easily lend itself to friendships. Our friends are either deathly afraid we will write about them or terribly bored at hearing the same subject discussed from all possible points of view. It's what writers do—talk. I think I am pretty ordinary. I think if I was looking for somebody to hang out with I'd be the last person I'd choose. There is a mirthful side to my personality and I basically like to laugh, but mostly I take things pretty seriously. A friend of my mother's was having dinner with us recently and we began discussing movies, which frankly I think of as a pretty safe topic. I kept saying, "What was the intent of that scene?" and she kept trying to tell me why she laughed. She finally said, "I know your problem! You're an intellectual!" Not really. I just think things should mean something and I get confused when there is no meaning to be found. We waste too much, we humans, because we refuse to recognize that there is a possibility of order and things making sense and we as a planet doing better.

I really don't know what to say about myself. I like music. There is something very special about capping my headphones and drowning in a vision of sound. Someone once asked me if I played an instrument and I replied, "My stereo." It's not surprising that man's first musical instrument was a drum; the image of the heart had to be manifest. The African people made use of the ability of the drum to both inform and incite; for over two hundred years of the American experience drumming was outlawed. A people, though, are rarely stopped in their legitimate desire for either knowledge or pleasure. Whether the Eighteenth Amendment would outlaw alcohol or the Miss America Pageant would desire the clothing of their Black Venus, a people, through individual risk or simply aesthetic innocence, will bring word of a new day.

It is sheer folly to assume the various African cultures were without stress, frustrations, discriminations. It is only our desire to escape the challenges of our own times that leads us to envision some African Eden with fruit dripping from every branch, fish jumping in clear cool ponds, women willing with no discernible persuasion, men strong, beautiful and capable after undergoing some variation of initiation into "manhood." If the human species alone among the mammals is capable of dreaming, we are also alone in our capacity for fantasy. America did not invent the blues for Africans—it simply made us sing them in English.

The giraffe alone, among those who are warm-blooded, is without a voice. All other mammals, most insects and, as we have learned to listen to the ocean, not an inconsiderable number of fish make some sound. Among those on earth the chirping of birds is universally considered pleasant, the howl of a single wolf on a mountain ridge the most mournful. We howl with the wolf not so much in imitation of his sound as in sympathy with another motherless child. The African slave bereft of his gods, his language, his drums searched his heart for a new voice. Under sun and lash the African sought meaning in life on earth and the possibility of life hereafter. They shuffled their feet, clapped their hands, gathered a collective audible breath to release the rhythms of the heart. We affirmed in those dark days of chattel through the White Knights of Emancipation that all we had was a human voice to guide us and a human voice to answer the call.

Anthropologically speaking, humans were divided in the workforce by gender. The men became the stalkers of prey; the women tended the fire, garden and children at the home site. Men learned at a very early age the value of quiet; women learned the necessity of talk. Men learned to compete for the best spot, the biggest share; women learned to cooperate, to socialize. If there was a benefit of slavery to the slaves it was that it broke down gender barriers; men and women shared the work, learned the songs, began and ended the day together. If there was a benefit to white people during the Great Depression it was that men learned how to deal with enforced idleness; women learned having a "good marriage" would not protect them from the reality that everyone has a right, if not an obligation, to do productive work.

It is historically considered that there have been two American revolutions: the one against the British for the right to tax ourselves and the one against the South to free chattel slaves. The revisionists consider there was perhaps a third revolution: the recovery from the Great Depression to meld compassion with free enterprise. Those of my generation know there has been a fourth: American youth, not with fife and bugle but with drums and boogie, headed for the twenty-first century with the battle cry: "Oo Whoop Baba Loo Boop Oo Whop Bam Boom!"

The Coasters said they'd been "Searchin'," and once again an African–Afro-American ritual—the Stomp—was being practiced. Anytime that song hit the airwaves Black youngsters would pour from their cars to form a big boss line. James Brown begged "Please Please Please" and the Midnighters informed us "Annie Had a Baby." Sam Cooke intoned "You Send Me," but the Dominos were only a "Sixty-Minute Man." Jesse Belvin said "Good Night My Love" but the Dells asked "Why Do You Have to Go?" The Brown decision was rendered by the Supreme Court and Eisenhower had a heart attack. In the heart of Black America it finally was made clear that no matter what we did, no matter how much we abided by the rules and regulations, no matter how straight our hair, correct our speech, circumscribed our behavior, no matter *what*—we were, in the words of Moms Mabley, "still a Negro."

The advantage to a people who have clearly defined an issue is this: The individual is relieved of the burden of carrying his people forward. He can dance upon his own floor in his own style. Though white Americans would try to this very day to make Black Americans responsible for each other, Black people recognize that just as individual accomplishments open no doors, individual failures close off no avenues. The Right Reverend Ray Charles said it best: "Tell the Truth!" We no longer were ashamed of being Black; we no longer wished to hide our love of chitlins and hog maws; we no longer wished to pretend we cared. Rosa Parks in Montgomery said "No!" and Chuck Willis asked "What Am I Living For?" Johnny Ace, who allegedly shot himself backstage at Houston's City Auditorium, went number one in England the next day with "Never Let Me Go;" Jesse Belvin's car blew four tires, killing him after he played a dance in L.A.; Chuck Willis died; Sam Cooke was murdered in L.A.; Frankie Lymon left the Teenagers to begin his involvement with drugs; Little Willie John was arrested for murder and died in prison; Otis Redding's plane crashed. Don't send me Murray the K as some kind of friend, let alone god to rhythm and blues. We paid for that music. Mr. K changed his Cleveland station format because Black and white kids were tuned to WCIN in Cincinnati, WDIA in Memphis, WDAS in Philadelphia and all night long WLAC in Nashville where "Randy" played and packaged the hits.

Black people had some place to run! We, like Max Schmeling, lacked a place to hide. We went "Dancin' in the Streets" behind Martin Luther King, Jr., behind Malcolm X, behind mighty mighty Sly and the Family Stone. If they snickered when Little Richard brought his painted lips, mascaraed eyes, hair piled high on his head out of his closet, they were silent when Cassius Clay echoed, "I'm Black and I'm proud." Otis Redding cried for "Respect," a coda to Chuck Berry's anthem, "Roll Over, Beethoven." And in case the message was missed, Aretha covered both Redding and Sam Cooke: "A Change Is Gonna Come." But Lady Soul, ever the lady, softened it with "A woman's only human." The Intruders replied, "Gotta let a man be a man."

I'm an old unrepentent rocker who joins with Bob Seger in demanding "Old-Time Rock and Roll." I've never been asked to do a commercial, but even if I were I couldn't demand "my MTV." No way. I like my music in my head and, when I was younger, my foot on the pedal. One of life's great thrills is putting Little Richard on the auto-reverse cassette in your car and heading from New York to Cincinnati. You don't even see the Jersey Turnpike. You pull over in Pennsylvania just before the first tunnel and get an orange sherbet ice cream from Howard Johnson's and you don't tune down until you creep through West Virginia. I liked being young and I like being not young. At the risk of being very, very dull I agree that "to everything there is a season." I think I would classify myself as happy. Which in no way means I don't go off on people, myself, situations . . . but more, that given a choice there wouldn't be too much too different in my life.

I'm finally old enough to know it would be nice to have money, but it's not all that necessary. I think I'd be a good rich person.

At least I know I would enjoy my money. Nothing galls me more than somebody who's come into some sort of fortune or been born to one bitching that life is hard. I'm sure life is since the end of life for all of us is death. It just seems unfair when you keep hearing people who can call long distance and talk as long as they like, who don't worry how their children's tuition will be paid, who don't fear for their health since they are properly insured going on and on about life's difficulties. It's tacky. The very least the rich can do for the rest of us is either enjoy or shut up. But what does that have to do with what I have written? Nothing.

I can think of nothing less interesting to me than to walk slowly through my poetry and say ". . . and then I wrote . . ." The books stand on their own. They will either live or die. I hate that pretentiousness of writers who think people are too dumb to understand what is being discussed. I lecture part of the year and it's a great joy to me. I like to meet people and I like to talk. I don't like to fly, but there are few college campuses that will agree to come to Cincinnati so I grit my teeth and go. The one thing I'm very conscious of is not going over very old ground. I'm a space nut so I do talk about space a lot; I'm into the Global Village, but mostly I try to bring the best of me to my audience. Even if it's not good it's honest. I simply refuse to believe the public has nothing better to do than come out on a cold night to hear me read a paper that could have been slipped under their door when the morning milk was delivered. The whole point to being "Live and In Person" is that you bring a live person.

Academia is such a controlled situation, people like me cause problems. I think speeches and fruit should always be fresh. I know, sure I do, that there are those who will say, "Well, what about dried fruit? I like dried fruit." This is not against dried fruit. A little Stilton on dried apricots is one of the taste treats of the world. Maybe a bowl of hot garlic soup followed by a roasted lamb shank and hey, you've got something. Yet one should always consider that fresh has its charm.

I'm just not a star. I think about it a lot. I say to myself: "Giovanni, be demanding. Make them put Perrier on the platform. Refuse to sign autographs when Saturn is in the house of Mars. Be peculiar. Get your makeup together. Need to change several times during your appearance. Demand a better dressing room. Keep people away. Work on your sneer. Practice hurting their feelings. Need special foods. Do something so folks will know that you know that they should know that you are special." Yet I distrust in the human species the need to exalt. Writing is like any other endeavor. I hope I am always able to bring my best to any audience that is kind enough to share an evening with me. I'm not humble. This is no Nikki Washington Carver. I believe in myself. I believe in what I do. Yet people need both gentleness and a challenge. Our college students especially need someone to talk to them as if they had sense.

I would remind any program chairman that it's *your* program. While it is unreasonable to ask your speaker to go to bed with you, it is not a burden to ask your speaker to have dinner with the committee. Your speaker has a right to be picked up on time. You have a right to a press conference. If your speaker is a funny eater, he should provide the food he needs. You provide what you can. And I'm not saying be sloppy. I don't care for McDonald's or Pizza Hut, but if that's what you can offer, then my job is to help you feel good about it while refusing to eat. I'm only your speaker for a short while. I will not try to change your habits if you don't try to change mine. I smoke. Anyone who picks me up after an airplane ride will find themselves facing cigarette smoke. That's because I don't drink. If you hate smoke, do not pick up your speaker. But hey, Miss Manners covers all this so much better than I. Your speaker at her best is there to serve you. If you are positive, she will be. If you are clear, she will relax and trust you. Should you also happen to know what your speaker does for a living ("Are you going to sing tonight?") you will win her affection ("No. I don't sing"), and pretty please don't decide to be honest ("Frankly I was hoping they wouldn't invite you") because that will depress your speaker ("But aside from that, Jackie, how did you like Dallas?") and she will become very closed instead of very open. Recognize that she is a human being whose dog may be sick, whose son has a science project due, who had water in the basement this morning when she left for the airport. Assume that she wants to be there and let her know you are pleased. Happiness is just such a nice thing to share. Try it. It may just make your day, too.

I date all my work because I think poetry, or any writing, is but a reflection of the moment. The universal comes from the particular. I like the nuts and bolts of life. I want to know everything. Sometimes, especially in the fall, if you're a morning person you wake up around five-thirty in the morning and start your coffee. The dark is just beginning to lift and in my backyard the birds come to drink and bathe. Soon they will not come so early because it will be too cold. But now they come and chirp. There's a big German shepherd that roams the neighborhood that is usually passing. But mostly you hear nothing. The sun rises in my eastern window where I am growing African violets and I just like to watch the red break and wonder about all the world. There is an ad concerning space that asks, "How long do we have to look at an organism before we recognize it?" How many little boys chunked the Rosetta Stone into the Red Sea before someone recognized that that was the key? And if there is never an answer, the quest is so worthwhile.

I like lace handkerchiefs. I like to look at those my grandmother passed to my mother; they are beautiful. Someone, perhaps Louvenia, perhaps my great-grandmother Cornelia, hand-embroidered them. They are as delicate as a spider web, as strong as a silkworm's coccoon. I cry when I watch *Little House on the Prairie*. I like to be happy. And other than an occasional response to an infrequent query I don't contemplate my work. I do try to be a good writer. I believe that I bring my best when I try to share. It's an honorable profession. There are so many pieces to my puzzle, I have no interest in trying to judge what I have done; but only to try to do more. I like my awards and honors. I love it when people say they have read my poetry. I never make the mistake of asking if they understood what I was *really* talking about or if they *really* liked what I did. I just thank them because whether I disappointed or delighted them they took the time to be involved in my effort ... to explore with me ... to extend themselves to me as I have extended myself to them. It's lonely. Writing. But so is practicing tennis or football runs. So is studying. So is waxing the floor and changing the baby. So is life. We are less lonely when we connect. Art is a connection. I like being a link. I hope the chain will hold.

◆ ◆ ◆ ◆ ◆ ◆ ◆ ◆ ◆ ◆ ◆ ◆ ◆

AN ANSWER TO SOME QUESTIONS ON HOW I WRITE:
In Three Parts

PART I

It's always a bit intimidating to try to tell how I write since I, like most writers, I think, am not at all sure that I do what I do in the way that I think I do it. In other words, I was always told not to look a gift horse in the mouth. Melvin Tolson said it much more poetically: A civilization is always judged in its decline. One reason that America has, I believe, always preferred its writers dead is that not only can it then be determined what we wrote and why we wrote that way, but we are not there to change our minds or correct any misgivings. A writer like W. E. B. Du Bois will always create problems for the critical establishment because he lived too long. Just think of the great joy that would have attended his death had Du Bois had the good sense, if not the actual kind disposition, to die after *The Souls of Black Folks*. He would have been hailed as a great seer, a prescient individual; all schoolchildren, black or white, would have been required to read his books. But Du Bois lived on, and wrote more and more, for almost all the next century. He is now dismissed by the white establishment as a Communist, and the Black critical establishment, which at least pays lip service to him, can't make up its mind which *one* of his books it ought to read. Writers are not rewarded for a body of work. We all seem to prefer one or maybe two books from a writer. After that we begin to hear disclaimers about how the earlier books were better, more passionate, or whatever. Ralph Ellison is probably the prime example. He has become, by virtue of one book, "the dean of Black writers"; yet a Chester Himes who continued to write was ignored. Though when Himes was kind enough to relieve us of his great talent we will all in time stand around giving memorials to him, decreeing the awfulness of the establishment that it failed to recognize him. We too have failed. But then, the Black writers seem no more able to overcome the green monster than any other writers. We fail to cheer for one another for a variety of reasons that have nothing to do with the art of writing itself. The conflict is not in the doing but in the talking about . . . which is also why my speeches are in prose and my poems in poetry. I was taught you never send a green frog to do the work of a Black princess.

I'm not sure I have any moral or political compulsions. I have habits: I smoke cigarettes, I drink an incessant amount of coffee and I do pick my nose when I'm afraid. It's gotten so bad, in fact, that I now know that I'm afraid because I find myself picking my nose. I think that emerged from my fear of airplanes. I love to fly. In some lone masochistic way I would love to go to the moon. I certainly would actively seek and never pass on a chance to at least circle the planet. I have been religiously saving my money to take the SST, and each time it becomes affordable for me the dollar drops again. There seems to be no limit to the ends of racism in this country. I'm totally convinced that any Black women who consciously circled the earth, let alone landed on another planet, would have a very different view of the heavens as well as the meagerness of earth. I think Black people, and Black Americans especially, are the only people to really view earth from its proper perspective since we have no land that we can in any historical way call our own. I think at this bisection of time and space we are the ones uniquely prepared to accept life on another planet. I believe the poets are the proper people to send since we see love and beauty in the blooming of the Black community; power in a people whose only power has been the truth. Maybe that's a compulsion. I like to tell the truth as I see it. I hope others do the same. That's why literature is so important. We cannot possibly leave it to history as a discipline nor to sociology nor science nor economics to tell the story of our people. As I understand "obviates," nothing obviates the political because the political embraces all the desires and history of the people. Perhaps someone will say, "Well, I think the history obviates the political." And I shall reply, "The only way you even know the word 'obviate' is that Mari put it on her questionnaire." If the politics of a people is only Democrat, Republican, Socialist, or even the Black political ideologies, then our people can be said to embrace no politics. Our politics have been the standing for that which is right and good; for the desegregation of society; for the equitable distribution of goods and services; for the free movement of a free people; for the respect for the old and the love of the young. Electing a few white boys or Black boys to office cannot be serious politics. Nothing significant changes whether the majority is white or Black, only the view. I support a Black view but let's not fool ourselves. The ideas and ideals that inform the Black struggles must always be the integrity of the human spirit. Can we really picture Martin Luther King, Jr., as a white man? White Americans have to go all the way back to John Adams or George Washington, and even they could fight their revolution with guns against soldiers who traveled thousands of miles across the sea. Our general had to use words against an enemy who lived next door. In the battle for peace the word will always be the winner. And we who are Black can never develop a love for rockets and planes and marvelous Titan missiles that go booooooom! in the night because a wrench fell on them. We must hunker down into that love of the spirit of Black Americans that allowed a janitor to be a deacon in a church or a washerwoman to sing that perfect note. We must, before we, like many an endangered species, become extinct, rediscover that we are Black and beautiful and proud and intelligent. I don't think everyone has to write the way I write nor think the way I think. There are plenty of ideas to go around. I just think that in life all things are political. What we do every day and how we do it. It's nice to love the people but it's necessary to be a friend to someone. Fanatics are, for one thing, boring and, for another, unreliable. They tend to burn out just when you need them. That's generally because they were, in essence, summer soldiers. When winter came they expected to be back home. I'm not against summer soldiers; they're better than none at all. But we need some long-termers too. All our enemies won't be as difficult and as easy as the Bull Connerses or the old George Wallaces. Some will be like Jimmy Carter; others won't even be white.

I don't feel besieged. I'm ever amazed at the idea that I am or can be anything other than what I am. If I'm not a Black woman then where is the real me? There used to be that old expression that you have two strikes against you: one as a Black and two as a woman. I never could quite understand what would make me strike out under those circumstances. I've always been a Black woman and I shall always be. I recognize the possibility that I may not always inhabit this body, since matter is neither created nor destroyed, leaving us all to understand that we are really nothing more than recycled matter from some other decaying thing. But why should I be different from any other thing on earth? What the plants expel, we inhale; what decays into the ground gives forth fruits and vegetables; when the glaciers pass, the lakes are formed. We don't ask the sun to consider the pleasures of the moon; why should female and Black humans be constantly asked how we feel about our essence? Those who ask are, in effect, trying to assure themselves that they are inherently better off to have been born male and preferably white. That's just so much tommyrot. I wouldn't be other than what I am because for one I can't; I can only fool myself into thinking that I can. And for two: I like myself.

PART II

My first nationally published article appeared in the now-defunct *Negro Digest* through the intercession of the late David Llorens. Either he thought I showed talent or he was being exceedingly kind to a young Fiskite and he purchased my first article. It made my day. There are probably no words to describe the joy you feel when you see your first words in print. There's a story that I probably shouldn't share about John Killens, who was at that time the writer in residence at Fisk, and me. When my article in the *Negro Digest* debuted John took me and the rest of the writing class out to dinner to celebrate. John had just purchased a new car. I left my copy of the magazine on his seat when we all got out at the restaurant and John went to park. When we came out John couldn't remember where the car was parked and, as he tells the story, my first words were, "Oh my God, my article is in the car!" John was, understandably from his perspective, more concerned about his new automobile. My point of view was, however, not wholly without merit. Your first published article is indeed quite precious. My first published book was done by a few friends and me. It was the book *Black Feeling, Black Talk*. I formed a publishing company, borrowed heavily from family and friends, and hired a printer. Luckily there were a number of Black bookstores around the country to which you could just send books: Ellis's in Chicago, Micheaux in New York, Vaughn in Detroit, and one in San Francisco. All were very kind to me and all paid me promptly. Then came the second wave of bookstores in the middle sixties, so it wasn't very hard to at least get a hearing on the merits of the writing. Now, of course, there are just too many chains, whether in bookstores or with publishers. The independents are all but gone and even those who hang on find distribution a major problem. I don't know if it's necessary for me to say, and those who are already aware can skip this part, but with an estimated twenty million Blacks we could control the best-seller list. There should be at least several books on the fiction and nonfiction best-seller list every year. I was so happy when *Song of Solomon* was acknowledged but also should have been *Just Above My Head*. I happen to write in an area where we are not charted so it's not at all personal. But Black writers are the only ones telling anything near the truth in either fiction or nonfiction. If Studs Terkel can make it so should *Drylongso*. But we all know Blacks don't like to purchase books. Though we should. The literature tells so much about our people. I hope the poetry too. I think we as writers don't have a true sense of our profession . . . that we are there to cheer each other on . . . to expose our people to and interest others in our works. There is, quite simply, too much jealousy in the profession . . . and we all suffer from it.

Every time I sit down with my typewriter I am beginning to write. The "beginning" cannot be told until I know the ending. I am, however, a writer very much grounded in my sense of place. I need my own coffee cup, my own chair, but most especially my own typewriter. I had a steam pipe burst in my apartment and my typewriter was uncovered and thereby ruined by the steam. I had had that typewriter since college. It was almost a year before I would even begin to touch this one. I think, by the way, that every intended writer should learn to type. Most of us have a poor handwriting, and thinking on a typewriter is different from thinking on a yellow pad. The sooner you can think on a keyboard, the less room you have for procrastination. And all writers are great procrastinators!

A more legitimate question might be, is there any room for white men in literature? Black women on both sides of the Atlantic are keeping traditional Western literature alive. We have, in Africa, Bessie Head, who with *When Rain Clouds Gather* and *Maru* has proven herself one of the great African writers writing in the English language, and, of course, Toni Morrison in the United States. Compared to what? Norman Mailer? Philip Roth? Be serious! *Roots* was of course a great popular success, though marred by the various controversies. I would hope each and every woman who ever thought she wanted to write would at least give it a try. It's not a ladder that we're climbing, it's literature we're producing, and there will always be someone to read it. The difference between young Black women and young Black men, as I see it, is that young Black men don't feel they will lose face if they say they want to write whereas young Black women aren't at all too sure that writing isn't too aggressive. What you hear a lot is: Can you write and be a good wife too? That's not exactly the question but that's what it amounts to. And the answer is probably no. Writing is a tough mistress, according to the men who've written about it, and I would submit it's no easier a paramour. But I'm not the best woman to ask about the blending of art and traditional married life because I think traditional married life is for traditional people. Or as they say in the Daily Ohio Lottery, "If you got it, go get it." I really don't think life is about the I-could-have-beens. I could have been a professional ballplayer but I met your mother; I could have been a professional dancer but my mother didn't want me to go to New York; or any variation of the theme. Life is only about the I-tried-to-do. I don't mind the failure but I can't imagine that I'd forgive myself if I didn't try. I don't have a life-style, I have a life. And I've made it a point not to analyze myself. I'll tell a story or confess a weakness but who I really am keeps surprising me. There's so much to learn about the species. I think it's foolish to determine what your life will be before you've even had a chance to live it.

PART III

Like all people who pry, I resist questions about my own work. I like to think that if truth has any bearing on art, my poetry and prose is art because it's truthful. I say that while recognizing that every time a truth is learned a new thesis, synthesis, antithesis is set in motion. I like to think I've grown and changed in the last decade. How else could I ask people to read my work or listen to me? It would have been pointless for a girl born in Knoxville, Tennessee, reared in Cincinnati, Ohio, to have lived in New York and traveled the face of this earth not to have changed. That would be an ultimate betrayal of the trust people put in any writer. I should hope there will be a body of work by Nikki Giovanni that's not just a consistency of unformed and untested ideas that I acquired somewhere in my late teens or early twenties. I seek change for the beauty of itself. Everything will change. The only question is growing up or decaying. We who are human have a great opportunity to grow up and perhaps beyond that. Our grasp is not limited to our reach. We who are writers live always in the three time zones: past, present, and future. We pay respect to them all as we share an idea. I loved my profession well before I joined it. I have always been a lover of books and the ideas they contain. Sometimes I think it is easy for we who write to forget that that is only half the process; someone must read. Now someone will say, "See, you have to cater to the audience!" But it's been my reading of history and understanding of politics that there is an audience for everything. If there is truly a sucker born every minute then perhaps we must wait the hour or the day for the wise one, the compassionate, the sensitive, for truly, the greater of the species appear to be in short supply, and yet they do come. There is always someone to remind us that there must be more to living than what we currently see. And that unusual person is what we seek. The bright, the concerned, the capable, are a part of our audience also. Someone said in the next century everybody will be famous for fifteen minutes. Who cares? We live now. As best we can. And we encourage others. We write, because we believe that the human spirit cannot be tamed and should not be trained.

◆ ◆ ◆ ◆ ◆ ◆ ◆ ◆ ◆ ◆ ◆ ◆ ◆

ABOUT
A
POEM

*A*s a child of the sixties I well remember when our movement began to sour. It isn't difficult to pinpoint. Some
people would like to say we soured when violence came into the
community and we began burning down our own homes and
businesses. I don't think so. We, both Blacks and whites, are a
violent people who throughout the American years have burned
both our own and any other available community. We kill each
other, we Americans, at a very high rate, whether at the stockade
or the stock market. We, as an African people, have a bloody
history of war. When I used to hear speakers of the sixties stand
up for Black Power I always considered it one up for a library
card because obviously they had just discovered something. Any
cursory reading of African history teaches us there is not now
nor has there ever been a dearth of warriors. The fact that a battle
or a war has occasionally been lost does not detract from the
ferociousness of the battle. There are some missing years because
our African ancestors were either unable or unwilling to protect the great libraries of Timbuktu and Alexandria. More likely,
given the human components, those who were not allowed to

partake of the knowledge refused to die to perpetuate it. But that is speculation on my part. What we do know and can easily see is for those of us who are Black Americans, both our African mother and our European father have never hesitated to use any and all destructive weapons—whether food or shelter; whether napalm or Agent Orange; whether selling a captive into slavery or keeping him as a POW in a tiger cage—to have their way. No. It could not have been violence in the late sixties that tempered the gains of the fifties and early sixties. Rap Brown teaches us "Violence is as American as cherry pie" and he could have added as African as the Click Song.

We did, however, learn something interesting about violence during the sixties. It doesn't work. Violence is like money in the bank; it's only helpful if you don't have to use it. Any of us who have any kind of little chicken-scratch bank accounts know exactly what I mean. It looks good to say, "I saved five hundred dollars during the past year." Now that's not a lot of money but it projects a certain image. You look a little more solid than the person who has saved nothing. If you play your cards right you can parlay that into another $500 and pretty soon you look good enough to get real credit. But if you have the money and take it out, even if you try to put it back, that withdrawal stands and folks from whom you want to borrow need to know why you took it out. The worst thing that can happen is that you have to close the account because you are below the minimum. Violence is like that $500. Once you use it you have nothing to fall back on and you have to start resaving and rebuilding. Our community had nothing to rebuild with, and a few loud mouths refused to understand that we had no additional funds. The Black community, as we look at the eighties, has had our account stamped "Closed." We are still trying to spend what we earned and had saved during another era. Were we formerly rich and decadent we could sit and discuss the "good old days," building poems and plays around our lost innocence. But we were just hard-working people who fell into a Black depression and have not allowed ourselves the time and energy to discover the "why" of our condition, therefore depriving ourselves of the tools to bring ourselves out.

We soured, this Black community, when we turned our backs upon who we are and who we could become. We have not been, historically, a community that has received help from the majority of our fellow citizens. We are really hard-pressed to find a time that the majority was committed to us. Sure there are statues to Abraham Lincoln but we didn't build them. If we were building statues we should seriously consider a railroad engine, for I much doubt that slavery would have had to go had it not been for Western Expansion. I know that's depressing to some people. Some of us want to think that people do the right thing for the right reason, but there is no history of mankind showing that. People do the best thing for the most expedient reason, and should there be a beneficial side effect we are all glad. It's just sad to think that somewhere in some big city or on some rural farm there is a gathering of Black folk wearing their pointed-toed shoes and little green caps agreeing with Peter Pan that they should never grow up. The reason we grieve when a child dies is not that we miss the child but that we mourn for the potential. Everybody should have an equal opportunity to grow up ... and grow old. It's not promised—tomorrow never is—yet it is adulthood that we seek. Somewhere during the sixties, Magic came into our movement.

People began to believe that if they wished hard enough everything would be all right. If they only wanted it badly enough their lives would turn around and they would be happy. Somehow Freedom, which is clearly a list of responsibilities, became a list of wishes. We began to sour. I remember the speeches exhorting the audience to turn their backs on the Uncle Toms, the church, their parents. As if that which was denying us Freedom was outside ourselves. As if people could deny or grant Freedom. The community turned it's back on the Freedom, since 1619, that we had achieved not only for ourselves but for the world. We, as a people, had so clearly shown that though our bodies were captured, our souls were free; that we could live with those who had so "dispitefully used us"; that though our bodies were tired "our souls were rested." The entire planet needs to take note of the Book of Black America because we rewrote the history of mankind when we neither fled our former captors nor sought vengeance. We showed that the human spirit had evolved.

But life is frequently like a chess game; for every step forward there are two to the side. We achieved true Freedom for those who had oppressed us and turned our backs on those who had freed us—the old men and women who had worked the fields; the young couples who built homes; the folk who insisted upon going into places where Blacks were not wanted; the students who studied to have skills; the businesspeople, both men and women, who not only serviced our community but employed our young; the old people who gave their dimes and dollars to build beautiful churches; the schoolteachers, beauticians, barbers, mailmen who through their Black Greek-letter organizations gave scholorships for young people to go to school; the men who did not abuse and desert their families; the wives who overlooked more than any woman should have to overlook. We soured because we failed to honor our forefathers. We wanted Freedom to be so much more than paying our bills at the end of the month; seeing our children grow up and go to college; retiring after twenty years on the same job. We wanted Freedom to be some kind of emotional lottery where when our number came up we would be rich and famous. We wanted Magic, and we soured because Freedom is reality.

I wrote a poem, *Nikki-Roasa*, in 1969 because you could see it coming. You could see the Government studies on the Black family and you could see the cavalry was on its way. My limited sense of Indian history taught me that any time the cavalry rides the natives had better scatter. You could see the "tender concern" for our Black youth and you knew: We would be the losers. The folks with the loud mouths and nothing in the bank thought they were winning: The Government was going to DO SOMETHING. Violent voices and violent acts thought they had carried the day. But nonviolence was never for the oppressor; it was for the oppressed. Martin Luther King's words were not to comfort the segregators but to teach us: If we can forgive them, we must then love ourselves. No one can be blamed for what he did not see, but we all bear responsibility for what we do not see. The magic of the Black community is ourselves. We held together when all others had fallen apart. We persevered as a community, in our families, when others turned their backs on us. We achieved from those segregated schools, diligently learning skills we had no forseeable opportunity to use; gaining strength in those churches built penny by penny from folks who were insulted daily while washing clothes and floors, hopping bells in hotels though they had college degrees, being called "boy" though the gray in their hair belied the summons. We had dignity in segregation and we must achieve dignity in Freedom. I fully recognize a poem is not a response to a report by the United States Government. I know a few words scribbled on a legal pad cannot turn anything around. Yet I wanted to say, as the old gospel song so aptly expresses, "It is well . . . with my soul." I wanted to say that an outhouse, that a lack of some toys sometimes did not destroy my family. I wanted to say, for those of us whose fathers took them for Sunday rides in the better communities, that knowing there is more in life does not mean we were less. We had each other; and we had our dreams. And we knew our dreams were not and could not be separated from the "each other." I wanted to say, in 1969, because you could see we as a community were missing something, that "Black love is Black wealth." And the riches we gain, having not been given by man, can never, by man, be taken away.

♦ ♦ ♦ ♦ ♦ ♦ ♦ ♦ ♦ ♦ ♦ ♦ ♦

FOUR
INTRODUCTIONS

♦ ♦ ♦ ♦ ♦ ♦ ♦ ♦ ♦ ♦ ♦ ♦ ♦

♦ ♦ ♦ ♦ ♦ ♦ ♦ ♦ ♦ ♦ ♦ ♦ ♦

A RIBBON
ON THE
MAYPOLE
(for Paule Marshall)

We can explain the generosity of the sun . . . by talking of expanding gasses . . . We can chemically legitimize water . . . as the union of hydrogen and oxygen . . . We can see a definite . . . undeniable . . . urge for flowers to turn to any source of light . . . But that is only observation of behavior . . . We also know slaves . . . identified with masters . . . that Jews . . . cloved to authority . . . that women still love men . . . So much of knowledge is not only empirical . . . but axiomatic . . . Yet the scientific gathering of data speaks exclusively to craft . . . There must also be art . . . if we are to yield reason

Anthropologically speaking . . . we are incorrect to accept the concept . . . that human male stood . . . to weld and brandish weapons . . . A more gentle data would allow us security . . . in the reasoning . . . that human female stood . . . to nurture and embrace . . . Psychologically speaking . . . we are unimpressed . . . that human genes are the determinant . . . of human responsibility . . . We would agree . . . rather . . . with the American Constitution . . . that all peoples are created equal . . . and are endowed with the inviolate right . . . to perceive the limitlessness of their possibilities unencumbered . . . by another's view of racial characteristics . . . gender responsibilities . . . or religious comforts . . . Law demands that we refrain from unacceptable behavior . . . Justice whispers to us the necessity of risk

We are not so different . . . we in this last quarter of the twentieth century . . . We congratulate ourselves on our military power . . . yet Alexander of Macedonia was bored . . . by his ability to conquer the known world . . . While debating issues of sustaining life or accepting death . . . it is the Oath of Hippocrates . . . to which our healers must adhere . . . We are justifiably proud . . . of our ability to penetrate the solar system . . . yet it was the priesthood of Egypt . . . which first calcuated the position of Earth . . . in relationship to the stars . . . Our arrogance of opulence pales . . . beside the splendor of Pompeii . . . our libraries no more than an afterthought to the great storehouses of Timbuktu . . . Our indifference to human suffering was as obvious in Imperial Rome . . . as the futility of fighting machines . . . was made clear to eighteenth-century London

To those who ask . . . in this space-age . . . high-tech . . . fast-paced . . . materialistic . . . immediately gratifying society of ours . . . what is the purpose of art . . . We would reply cavewoman has answered that question . . . In defiance of damp cold and dark habitat . . . against men and animals who would make of her their evening meal . . . despite a lack of adequate tools or knowledge of their proper application . . . on clay walls . . . in tune with the rhythm of her crackling fire and crying babies . . . she took the time to sketch a saber-tooth . . . to etch the power of a mammoth . . . to exhibit awe . . . that the sun warms . . . the waters flow . . . the winds bend trees

We turn to literature . . . for the emotional gathering of data . . . not to say that war still occurs . . . but to show the continuing human price for human impatience . . . Not to show that hunger still exists . . . but to exacerbate unremitting greed from human relationships . . . Not to erect signs saying: "Mine" . . . but to wrap a ribbon on the maypole . . . We turn to literature . . . because our greatest literature teaches us "in the beginning was the Word . . ." . . . And it is the word that will lift the ignorance of the dark ages from our spirits and cast our possibilities to the heavens . . . It is words that will set us free

♦ ♦ ♦ ♦ ♦ ♦ ♦ ♦ ♦ ♦ ♦ ♦ ♦

"THE SPIRITUAL: EVOLUTION OF A PLAINTIVE MESSAGE"

There are advantages to slavery other than to the slave master. The slave master only gets free labor, and "free" only in the sense that there is no monetary exchange. The payment comes when the master has to surrender his soul to say that the enslaved is not human. The oldest book in the world asks: What profits a man if he gains the world but loses his soul? But the slave, and I am not recommending this system, learns that he can do that which, in contemplation, he thought impossible. He can survive, yes, thrive in a system that puts his total being under assault. All too many young people today look at the outward restraints, without understanding the inner strengths, that our people have endured.

All systems require myths for their longevity. One current myth that is working to the group advantage is that all Asian immigrants are smart; that they excel in science and math. One current myth working against our group is that we are lazy; that we only want welfare and special treatment. The problem with myths is that they are believed by both those for whom they work and those whom they work against. No slave was ever lazy; for he would not survive. No slave ever shied from hard work; for he did as he was told.

No slave was ever stupid—uneducated, certainly, but never stupid; for he not only had to understand what the overseer wanted but what he would settle for.

One myth that the American people like to perpetuate is that those who came to these shores, from the days of the ill-fated Jamestown settlement to the boat people from Haiti, came by choice. Hip liberals and sensitive conservatives like to concede that Black Americans are here against our will. That we are the only unwilling migrants to the New World; somehow putting us in a category that says since we didn't want to be here perhaps we would be better off somewhere else. If we are the only unwilling migrants, and the Native Americans the only natural inhabitants, then we both can be excluded from the American family. No place need be set at the table for the Black brother for as soon as he is able, he will go to his real home.

One is, of course, forced to ask what level of choice are we dealing with? Did the Black Plague of Europe constitute a "choice" when the options were death or migration? Did the religious persecution of the British and French constitute "choice" when a man was not allowed to follow the dictates of his heart? Did the rotten potatoes lying in Ireland's fields constitute "choice" when the options were starvation or migration? I suggest the Spaniard with the viciousness of the Inquisition had no more "choice" than the African captured by a rival ethnic group and sold to the slavers. No option, philosophy teaches us, makes the perfect choice. And imminent death presents no option.

We do not, and cannot, know what the African response to the New World would have been had we had different options. We do know that the Moors traveled to Spain and built some of the most beautiful buildings, stocked libraries, gave Spain the advantage of their mathematical prowess. We do also know America could not be the same without us. There are legitimate Black complaints that in the Middle Passage we lost our native language, our cultural roles, much of our ethnic identity. We also became a new people with a new song.

We worked together, showing both ourselves and others that ethnicity is not a necessary ingredient for human relationships. We accepted new gods and found unique ways of worshipping while building tolerance for those who believed differently and those who did not believe. We were slow to judge as we understood that the burdens of mankind weighed differently upon different shoulders. We cultivated the land, built the bridges, painted the portraits, laid out Washington, D.C., performed the first open-heart surgery, separated the plasma from the blood, made the first shoe lasts, and did more things with a peanut than anyone could imagine.

But more than our material contributions, which, like the Rock of Gibraltar, though still standing, is just sand, we stood firm and fast for the reality that every man is equal in the sight of God and must be respected under the Laws of Man. We know, we who labored under the lash, that though our bodies were tired, our souls were rested. We willingly gave the world our song, which Dvořák made into his *New World Symphony* and we made a daily part of our lives.

In this, the fifth year of the Spiritual Festival Competition, I am proud to join the Human Involvement Project in celebrating "The Spiritual: Evolution of a Plaintive Message." Five years ago, when the Human Involvement Project was told its funding would be severely limited, that it might not be able to go forward with its work of serving people, a vow was made not to descend to despair but to climb to higher ground. The Human Involvement Project reached deep into its soul to rediscover that which had carried our ancestors over—a song. A new song for a new day. We are now celebrating a dream that was dreamed not on our backs, in our beds, with the curtains drawn to shut out the light; but a dream that was realistically dreamed of determination and self-help.

I am especially proud to be honorary chair in this anniversary year, believing as I do that "Without a song . . . there ain't no love at all . . . without a song."

◆ ◆ ◆ ◆ ◆ ◆ ◆ ◆ ◆ ◆ ◆ ◆ ◆

THE WOMEN'S ALLIANCE

(Introduction to Mari Evans)

The giraffe is the only species without a voice. We share with the dolphin identifiable laughter. We recognize and give integrity to the language of the apes, baboons, orangutans and other primates though we cannot translate it. We understand and appreciate the growls and howls of the wolves, hyenas, lions, tigers, our own pet dogs and cats. Yet human beings are the only species with codifiable language.

What joy that first human must have experienced when sound, reproducible sound, came from his throat. Did he howl in imitation of the wind; did he chirp with delight at a bird; did he laugh and gurgle like the stream? He probably pointed and made a sound. And someone pointed and made a sound back.

Language builds from necessity. Only recently have we invented microwave, electric boogie, radar, penicillin, supersonic transport, superstars. Our technology has afforded us a new lease on life, so terms like "death with dignity," "sexual preference," "artificial intelligence" and "single by choice" have become necessary to explain ourselves to ourselves. Most people recognize Acquired Immunity Deficiency Syndrome or herpes, though they react to those words as if it was still B.C. and thereby interchangeable with "leper." Mankind has learned a lot but we have not internalized the intent.

We have learned that separate is never equal and therefore cannot be separate. We have learned that quality education means young people can read, write, compute, and think with some logic. We have learned we cannot expect people to pull themselves up by their bootstraps ·then take the boots away; but those of us without shoes have also learned we must never cease marching forward—no matter what hardships we encounter.

One of the new terms is "role model." When people do not want to do what history requires, they say they have no "role models." I'm glad Phillis Wheatley did not know she had no "role model" and wrote her poetry anyway. I'm glad Harriet Tubman did not know she had no "role model" and lead the slaves to freedom. I'm glad Frederick Douglass did not know he had no "role model" and walked off that plantation in Maryland to become one of the great oratorical fighters for freedom. I'm glad Thurgood Marshall did not say the Constitution prescribes me as three fifths of a man therefore I cannot argue the Brown vs. Topeka case before the Supreme Court. I'm glad Martin Luther King, Jr. did not say but segregation is the law of the land and we cannot defy the law, but rather raised his voice in constructive engagement against the segregationist practices of our generation.

The power of speech, the freedom to engage our hearts and our bodies in dialogue is the most precious freedom of all. To secure all other rights granted to us by either our religions or our laws it is necessary to raise our voices. An idea inside our heads is, to our fellow humans, the same as no idea. It must be expressed if it is to have power. And the voice, the pen, is far mightier than any sword, any jail, any attempt to silence. Censorship is an anathema to a free people. We may not always like what we hear but we are always the poorer if we close down dialogue; if we abrogate free speech, and the open exchange of ideas.

A great part of the joy of being human is not that we think; many other mammals think. Nor that we communicate with our fellow mammals; all other mammals communicate inter- and intra-species; but that we have a history which is located in human memory and in books. We are not bound by the moment but can go back thousands of years to see how far we have progressed; and we can go forward in imagination to envision our future.

We with our history of slavery where native gods, language and drums were taken from us devised a language using the Christian tools available. They serve us well, giving voice to frustration; offering comfort to the aggrieved. Music is a universal language: The field hollers, the gospel calls to worship are universally recognized as a major Black contribution. Patience is universal: The faith of a mustard seed, the determination of one drop of water in the Grand Canyon, 'cause if Job waited on the Lord tell me why can't I? Love is universal because we recognize and accept the call to reconcile the irreconcilable. And books are our window to these worlds.

We are honored to have with us today a poet, a book maker, a window on the world. Ladies and gentlemen . . . Mari Evans.

◆ ◆ ◆ ◆ ◆ ◆ ◆ ◆ ◆ ◆ ◆ ◆ ◆ ◆

STAINED-GLASS
WINDOWS
(for Bobbi Sterne)

Patterns are usually found on material . . . making colors blend with colors . . . disimilar patterns form . . . new patterns . . . creating new styles . . . new fashions . . . new ideas: of what is chic . . . what is acceptable . . . what will be the future . . . Patterns are the way most lives are lived

Quilts are traditionally formed from scraps . . . pretty little left-overs . . . sewn painstakingly by hand under candlelight . . . or kerosene lamps . . . a communal endeavor with the ladies bringing their own pieces to share . . . carefully laying her contribution in just the right place at just the right time . . . Casseroles are quilts . . . different dishes on the same table . . . making a complete meal . . . for all the guests . . . Politics are quilts . . . each piece offering comfort to the old . . . disabled . . . the needy . . . as well as new responsibilities to the young . . . the able . . . those who know sufficiency . . . Quilters teach there is no such thing as waste . . . only that for which we currently see no purpose . . . Quilters teach patience to a hurried . . . impatient world

Stained glass is a colorful quilt . . . of processed sand . . . formed to keep the cold away . . . while allowing the light to come through . . . This is woman's work we are discussing . . . those who can see

... the beauty and majesty ... of that which has been left behind ... Those who know ... with their hands and their hearts ... that the little pieces need each other to make a different day

Even dark days ... even cloudy skies ... concede the majesty of stained glass ... a creation of an individual who said, "Let us not close up this space ... Let us also not let the naked wind blow through ... Let us take these broken pieces and form a pattern ... showing humans were here who used the leftover ... who eliminated the waste ... who did not through away the scraps ..."

Most artists ... even in our modern times of WASHINGTON SLEPT HERE ... and KILROY ... and TURK 182 ... are unknown ... laboring more for love ... than praise or money ... Those whose minds ... are more nimble than their hands ... weave a human quilt ... of little people ... bringing them together to fend against the naked winds ... of hopelessness ... despair ... a feeling of uselessness ... We who have admired ... the artistry of stern and patient weaving ... stop now among the shattered glass to admire the old patterns ... and to quietly ... and persistently ... pick up the pieces ... to make new stained-glass windows where the old were blown away

◆ ◆ ◆ ◆ ◆ ◆ ◆ ◆ ◆ ◆ ◆ ◆

THE
SPORTS
PAGES

◆ ◆ ◆ ◆ ◆ ◆ ◆ ◆ ◆ ◆ ◆ ◆

◆ ◆ ◆ ◆ ◆ ◆ ◆ ◆ ◆ ◆ ◆ ◆ ◆

Defend Yourself

Defend Yourself
Against
Your: Husband, Lover or Friend

Everything
you ever wanted to know
About Sports
but are too embarrassed
to ask

Nikki Giovanni
Famous Sports Fan and Poet will teach you
Terms—Tone—Techniques
to sound like you know what
you are talking about

A California Woman writes:
How do you know which sport
is being played?
Giovanni Answers:
If they are in their underwear—it's Basketball;
if they have on their pajamas—it's Baseball;
if they wear helmets—it's Football.

Don't YOU want to know Something
about Sports???

◆ ◆ ◆ ◆ ◆ ◆ ◆ ◆ ◆ ◆ ◆ ◆ ◆

MY
OWN
STYLE

I want to be a modern woman. I still have a nostalgic Afro, though it's stylishly short. I apologize to the hair industry, but frankly I like both my kinks and my gray strands. Plus being a sixties person glowing in the dark carries negative implications for me. The cosmetic people get my fair share. Most of my friends do base, pancake, powder, eye, lipstick and always keep their nails in perfectly oval shapes with base, color, sealer and oil for the cuticles. Do I use these things? No. But neither do I put them down or try to make them feel guilty for not being natural. There is something to be said for improvement. I've been known to comment: "Wow, you look really good. Who does your nails?" Why, I even have a dear friend who is a few months younger than I who uses a night cream to guard against wrinkles. Do I laugh and say, "You damned fool, you have no wrinkles"? No, ma'am. I say, "Well, your face is very very smooth," which (1) makes her feel good about her efforts and (2) keeps the friendship intact. All of life is a compromise anyway.

My major contribution to cosmetics is soap. I love soap . . . in pretty colors . . . hand-milled . . . in interesting shapes . . . with the name of good perfumers on them . . . preferably French. No one in my immediate family, and few who have ever used my bathroom, ever wonders what to give me for my birthday, Christmas, Valentine's Day, Mother's Day, Fourth of July, Labor Day, Martin Luther King, Jr.'s Birthday or Lincoln Heights Day. The way I figure, ask for what you want. I used it to, of course, bathe with, but it's also so pretty on my open shelves, plus it smells good and when properly arranged is more or less a living sculpture.

I really like useful things. You never know. Take candles. I really like a candle. I'm a Democrat so I have a donkey. I'm a Delta so I have an elephant. I'm a woman so I have an apple. Well, I have an apple candle; maybe I don't have to justify it. I also have candle candles. Just tall pretty candles in little holders. If the house gets hit by lightning I'm ready. Like all modern women I like to be ready. Without raising a hair on my chinny chin chin I can turn three cans of anything and a quarter cup of dry white wine into a gourmet meal in fifteen minutes flat. Give me an ounce of Cognac and I really raise hell. I've been known to make the most wicked bean soup with warm croutons and garlic zwieback (the secret is a dapple of sherry) the world has known. People say, "How can you be a full-time mother, full-time professional and still cook like this?" I smile sweetly, indicating that perhaps the very best is yet to come. Or as the old folk liked to say, "It ain't what you do, it's the way that you do it." In observing the younger women, that seems to be the one thing that they are missing: the ability to take nothing and make everybody think that something is there. You know what I mean? The younger women like to brag that they can't cook, as if that makes them modern. What is really modern is that you can throw it together from cans and frozen food and pretend that it was easy. Half of life is not avoiding what you don't like but doing it with no sweat.

I must congratulate the twentieth-century woman on her internationalism. You go into practically any house these days and they have Nigerian art, Egyptian cotton throws, French water, Hawaiian fruit, Japanese televisions, California wines, Polish crystal, Haitian lace curtains, Lesothan rugs, Dutch flowers sitting on their grandmother's handmade quilts draped across an Early American table. I think it's neat. There are no limits to our imagination. My house is a mess, too, so that means I qualify. Or as the lady who came to sell me draperies said: "It's not too many people who will put a print on a print." Well, it works. Mostly because I want it to work. And since it's my house . . . It's the little things that make the difference. I remember when you could go by the apartment of any guy of any relationship to you and find stale beer in the refrigerator. Nowadays even their places are perking up. Everybody wants to make a statement.

Oh sure, I've heard all the jokes about BUMPS (Black Upwardly Mobile Professionals), but I like a BUMP. Hell, I am one. Being laid back is a sexual term, not a personality description. We could use a little ambition in our community. Everytime somebody wants to trade their Toyota for a BMW that means they have to have more people to supervise; a bigger budget to spend; a larger program to implement. If they're in business for themselves they have to sell more, do more, 'cause everybody knows you don't get big in business by saving, you get big by spending, by expansion. I mean we are only fifteen years out of the twenty-first century! The Black community is 40 percent teenage unemployed, 53 percent illiterate. We are the most Social Security-froze, Medicaid-stopped, unwed, underemployed, unpromoted, not-appreciated-at-all community in America. Who we gonna call—Honkeybusters? No! We're gonna climb out on the BUMPS. The modern woman is a BUMP who is not a grind. We can do it 'cause we've done everything else. And hey, even though my body will be old sitting on a porch in some home, unless I can convince my son to let me live with him and his little wife (he does owe me, you know—I have given him right now fifteen years of my life and I expect the little bugger will be going around the block a few more times), I'll be surrounded by the good feeling that I am a modern woman 'cause even if I'm old I'm sure to be positive, and that's our ace in the hole.

♦ ♦ ♦ ♦ ♦ ♦ ♦ ♦ ♦ ♦ ♦ ♦ ♦ ♦

LET'S SWEAT!

*L*ike most poets, I carry a two-hole folder with me almost compulsively. It's not that I carry my ideas around so that should the occasion arise I can pull it out and say, in regard to some impending problem, "Oh well, a stitch in time saves nine." I do not have profound idioms at occasions of great distress so that I can intone: "It's always darkest before the dawn." No. It's just that like most writers I think I think best when I'm not actually thinking about it, so I carry a book that allows me to put either something I have thought up as being very clever or, most likely, something that someone else said that I would one day like to use. Steve Krieder, running back for the Cincinnati Bengals, once said in response to the question "Why do you think the fans came out in — twenty degree weather to watch a football game?" "I think it's a failure of our educational system." I think that is neat. I love sports, too; but any fool who would sit in Riverfront Stadium in twenty below-zero weather to watch a game that was being televised anyway indeed has been let down by our public school system. I haven't found a way to work that into a poem, but with any luck and lots of persistence I will ultimately be able to achieve it. You don't see too many good poems on football. Baseball has

"Casey At The Bat," but when you think sports, that's about it. Tennis needs a national poem. So does soccer. Any reader out there who's a soccer fan should really think about it because soccer is an international game and you could get a real chance to show off your Latin, Greek, Spanish, English, ancient Gaelic. It could be a real intellectual *tour de force*, as it were. I mention my folder because, in fact, I want to talk about sports. My folder, which is bright orange, has a mock license plate saying POETIC LICENSE, which is normal since I do poetry. But right below that is a white and orange circle that states: BODY BY SCANDINAVIAN. It's true. I've joined the Spa Revolution.

You may rightfully wonder why a forty-three-year-old woman would suddenly decide she can no longer get along without getting her body in shape. And that is exactly the point. If people know anything about the writing profession they know that all we do is sit and read or sit and write or sit and talk or sit on planes to go sit and do all of the above. I personally know writers whose legs give out if they have to go up one flight of stairs and now refuse to lecture at certain universities because the schools lack elevators. That's simply being in bad shape. Some writers have even given up smoking cigarettes, though I do not count myself among them, in the hope that they can avoid exercise. Dear young writer out there, you must sweat.

I guess you are wondering how I got into sports in the first place. I was visiting my father and mother one fall when a bunch of my dad's friends came over. Laughing loudly with beer and munchies they plopped themselves in front of the television and begin to talk in numbers and letters. RBI's 35; ERA 3.56; HR 15; only 21 percent against left-handers and other things I didn't understand. It seemed so unlike my father to have gone into the stock market. I went into the living room and asked what was going on. It was friendly. I mean, I wasn't meddling or anything—just curious. You know the look you get when people think you are not quite bright? well, five men turned to my father: "And that's the famous one, huh?" And they all burst out laughing. My father was mortified. "We're watching the World Series, sweetie," he said sweetly. That should have been my clue to go on, as he never called me "sweetie" unless I had done something extremely stupid and he was exercising great patience to not scream, "Lughead, what do you think is going on?" I then, with the smile, I'm sure, of the terminally stupid, asked, "Oh, who's playing?" The room literally shook with laughter. I, naturally, beat a hasty retreat. The Giovannis are a close but competitive family. I determined from then on that the next time I came to visit I would know the sport, who was playing and what all those little numbers meant. From then on instead of reading the front page I turned to sports first. I cribbed a *Sports Illustrated* anywhere I could. I even purchased *Sporting News* and, during Hagler's heyday (though the Marvelous One may think he is still in his heyday) read *Boxing News.*

Since I travel a lot I also made a great discovery. Alone in a hotel room on the road I would usually tune in *Tonight* or one of the talk shows. I can't stand violence and no lone woman in her right mind would look at *Hawaii Five-O* or any of those pictures where women are stalked and brutally killed. I learned, and I'm lucky cable came in when it did, that I could catch the West Coast games live. I'll bet I know more about the Phoenix Suns during that period than any poet from the East Coast. I do have to confess I never became a Lakers fan but I kind of appreciate Houston— unless they're playing the Celtics. I could come back to a cold, empty hotel room in the middle of February and tune in something to cheer about. I could catch boxing, West Coast tennis, gymnastics—hell, fencing, if it came to that. I never did get into hockey because my major sports requirement is that I have to be able to see the ball, but I'm working on golf. Ahhh, but bowling. I love to watch bowling. You get a big, usually black, ball going down a clearly defined lane. I could sit and munch Planter's peanuts and cheer my little head off. I'm sure many a night my next-door neighbors, as I screamed, "Oh yes! Go for it! Put it in now!" were green with envy at the dull, rather pedestrian happenings in their bedrooms. Sports is fun. We expect the men to want to go shopping to pick out curtains but we don't feel the same obligation to understand why you punt on fourth down. We want the guys to marvel at the cleanliness of our homes but we don't want to know what a cleanup hitter is. Come on, girls. Let's be fair. It's time to quit being jealous of our jogging mates and join in. Since we sweat anyway, sometimes it ought to be on our feet as well.

◆ ◆ ◆ ◆ ◆ ◆ ◆ ◆ ◆ ◆ ◆ ◆ ◆

TOWARD BETTER
HUMAN
UNDERSTANDING

O K, ladies, I'm going to help you out. I know I'm a poet and that poets are not supposed to be interested in these things, but let's file it under "Toward Better Human Understanding." That allows our subject to be considered either political or sociological. Men and women are different, and no matter what kind of data we uncover we will still see the differences . . . and sports proves it.

I'm not talking simple anatomy. Women, since the days of slavery, have been strong and physically capable, and we're not just discussing Black American slavery here. The Great Pyramids were as much built by female Jewish slaves as by male. The great Roman roads were laid by women and men. The stuff you see in movies and on television defies logic. The women were not simply lovingly dressed and taken into concubinage while the men gathered the straw. Both did bedroom duty; both did fieldwork. Black American slavery does at least openly admit women were worked like men, though I think the term is "worked like a . . ." (It's not, by the way, that I'm against using certain pejorative terms, but when every comedian and left-wing politician thinks he can show he's hip and prejudice-free by using the term it's time for those of us who had a more familial connection to desert the field.) Anybody who thinks the women who went West in covered and uncovered wagons to open the frontier just stayed around the home fire fretting about the town gossip and baking biscuits is nuts, too. We shot Indians, marauding Mexicans and crazy white men who bothered us. We tilled fields, harvested the crops, fought weather, loneliness and sometimes our mates—the same as we do today. The myth of the delicate woman is very recent and very inaccurate. You had your historical crazies like the Chinese peasants who bound the feet of their wives and daughters because the Chinese rich did it. Of course, the rich did it to show that they were rich. The poor did it in pitiful imitation of the rich. Foot-binding is as sick as the cry for virgin women. It's simply a sign of men talking to men. "Hey man, I'm so rich my ol' lady want to go someplace I have Chester, here, to carry her!" "Babe, you too much. Do she walk to bed or do he carry her there, too?" (With a lot of eye-rolling and back-slapping.) Like soft hands. Some pitiful woman married to a normal factory guy or schoolteacher or policeman for that matter is ex-pected to have hands that look and feel like she never washed a pair of socks or cleaned a greasy skillet or scrubbed the ring from around the tub. I mean, if you work with your hands, your hands will show it. And I say Hurrah. What a false sense of ego some men must have. How foolish of the women not to protest. All those overlong, splitting nails, patchy red-polished dishpan hands trying to make, hoping to believe, that Jergens or Palmolive or some miracle would make their hands be less red, less cracked, less dry. Scarlett should have said to Rhett, "There's a war going on, dummy. What the hell do you mean, what's wrong with my hands?" I'm simply trying to establish that women have used, and always will use, our bodies for real work. What we have been reluctant to use ourselves for is real play. Women don't like to sweat.

I do. I love sweat dripping from my chin or running down the back of my neck. I wear an Afro so I don't have to worry about my hairstyle. I can shower after a tennis match and wash my hair and go on about my business. In all fairness to the younger women, I'm also forty-three and figure what I haven't had I won't get. Athletics are fun. I've been totally cheered by the female body-builders. People thought they were nuts ("I don't see what they gonna do with all them muscles. No man ain't gonna want them"). Though those of us who have followed the history of men know men want any and every thing. My favorite sport is tennis, though as a two-pack-a-day smoker, I either have to win early or accept defeat graciously. I am, of course, very gracious. I bowl in the high 100's, of which I am very proud, and can run a quarter mile in fifteen minutes. I've even joined a spa lately, where I have been known on rare occasions to do ten sit-ups, though they are not my favorite. Aerobics. I like the music, the side-to-side motion, the look of my AMF red-velvet heavy hands flinging into space calorie after calorie, which are burned, incinerated, banished to that place where lost weight goes on hiatus until it finds another woman to descend upon. I've learned something else. Why men like to look at sports.

I need to take a minute to, if not explain something, then at least admit it. Since turning forty I have found that I drift off the subject. Many's the year I had to hear that I was too direct, without humor, did not see the shadings. It never used to bother me until I turned forty. I never used to cry at commercials either. I never used to get choked up at poignant endings. Just a few scant years ago I would have torn apart a movie like *The Trip to Bountiful.* I would have found the son too weak, the daughter-in-law too stark, the mother too much a caricature. But I watched that movie and threw popcorn at the screen screaming, "Let her sing a hymn!" I just couldn't take it. I should have known it was coming because I used to get tears in my eyes watching that kid take the shirt from the football player in that Coke commercial. I mean, the kid looked so happy to have that sweaty shirt and it was so sweet of the player to give it to him. All right, I'll admit it. A tear or two fell when Pete Rose broke Ty Cobb's record. It was so touching. I had to be helped from the room when that Swiss female marathoner,

Gabriele Anderson, limped crazily into the arena at the Los Angeles Olympics. "Don't touch her! Don't touch her!" I yelled until my mother, realizing I had once again been gotten to, put a steady hand on my elbow and took me into the kitchen muttering, "She'll be all right. She'll finish."

Unfortunately for me, my mother just loves *Little House*. Now, I can take the girls being blind and seeing again and all the fires and operations because I don't emotionally identify. But the show where the aging wrestler needs the money for his dying wife . . . well, I refused to look at it for the third time. It's just too much. I can't watch the *Highway to Heaven* where the actor ascends in front of the curtain to heaven after asking God to give him a sign that He understood the actor had tried to live a good life. It seemed that he asked for so little and it's only right that it be granted. And let's not even discuss *Star Trek*. The idea that Spock might die just broke me up. I had taken my son and two of his friends to see it and they all were horribly embarrassed by me. I got them back with *E.T.* Everybody heaved through that one. So I admit emotion has come into my life and, in many ways, I cannot control it. Honestly, I cried like a baby after amassing 346 points at Scrabble only to go down in defeat. But that's understandable. Most men like to watch sports because they refuse to admit they cry at commercials. They like to watch sports because they like to think that a group of men playing a game together are friends and really care about each other. They like to use terms like "Teamwork" and "I'll quarterback this" and "Let's run this up the middle" to get their subordinates to work harder. They sit around on Friday nights (fights), Saturday (college ball), Sunday (pro), and Monday (pro) wanting to believe that man does not struggle alone. That his fellows are there with him. That the team concept is alive and well. They cheer loudly and argue insistently about plays because it's also the only time they can show great and intense emotion without someone trying to analyze it. They can scream and holler and curse and thank the various deities without having to worry that someone will attatch any deeper meaning. They watch sports, ladies, for the same reason you watch *General Hospital, The Young and the Restless, Dynasty* and *Dallas.* They need a fantasy. One other thing I should mention. They like sports because they are the undisputed master of the ERA, at-bats, percentages against left-handers vs. percentages against right-handers. This from a man who cannot remember his anniversary and occasionally forgets his wife's name ("*Honey*, will you bring me a beer?") Something primordial and personal happens when a man watches sports. He doesn't have to talk to women.

Most women don't like to watch sports because we are jealous of the men enjoying themselves without our help. We hear the same animal grunts and groans, the same urgings to come on, to finish it off, as we hear in private moments, and women don't want to compete with the New York Jets for private moments. I'm surprised some mate has not reported his significant other as running into the room near tears during the Super Bowl saying, "But, Timothy, I thought that was our grunt." And in our genetic jealousy we seek, not understanding of our negative emotions, but excuses. "I don't like boxing," (with lips pursed) "because it's too violent." Have you ever been to a department store the day after Christmas? Have you ever been in any grocery store when 96-ounce Coke was announced as on sale for the next twenty minutes for 76 cents? Did you never seek a Cabbage Patch doll for your child or grandchild? How can women really discuss violence?

Boxing is a marvelous sport. Except for the heavyweights you have two wonderfully muscled men in the ring in shorts outpointing each other. Yes, I will admit that you sometimes find real hackers who are simply trying to hurt the other man, but real boxing— and we do have to look at the heavyweights now—is an art. You take Muhammed Ali who at the peak of his career raised boxing to liquid sculpture. No one would compare Ali to Sonny Liston, Joe Frazier or Larry Holmes, because they, as Ali liked to say, were just big bears. Sugars Ray, both Robinson and Leonard, were a joy to watch. And Michael Spinks has shown it's not size but skill. Will boxing learn Michael's lesson? Probably not. But when you see a Lonnie Smith, who unfortunately lost his title, you see a man moving with a purpose. But mostly, whether you or I or the American Medical Association like it or not, boxing is here to stay. Men will always test themselves against each other. Someone is bound to say, "But we don't have to support it . . . it's barbaric." So is the stock exchange; so are interest rates; so are farm foreclosures; so is life. Most women don't want to think that someone could really enjoy hitting or getting hit by someone else. It's probably quite fair to say no one enjoys getting hit. Hitting . . . well, that's another matter.

Football is fun, too. My sister once asked me, "Why do they get up close to each other and scrunch down?" I realized right away why she doesn't enjoy the sport. She doesn't know what's going on. My answer was, of course, a very patient, "I don't know." Because I don't. I'm not only not a sport historian, I don't intend to become one. They line up because that's the way the game is played. A better question, and one that can be quite a conversation opener, is, "Why don't they throw on first down?" Your significant other will try to explain the importance of establishing a running game, which can take up quite a bit of time. If you occassionally ask something like, "Well, why don't they go for it on fourth down and inches? That front line isn't all that tough," you can talk all afternoon. Do not, I repeat, do not ask that if his team is playing against the Chicago Bears. You will look like the imposter you are. With any other team it'll do just fine. One minor thing you need to know: The object of football is first downs—not touchdowns, first downs. Your mate will be perfectly happy to have his favorite team lose if they get more first downs. Now that may not make sense but I'm not trying to make sense, I'm trying to save your relationship.

Shortly before the actual close of football—well, truthfully before the World Series is played—the NBA will raise its head. If your spouse is not a football nut you can count on losing him during basketball season. The trick to understanding basketball is calling the foul. You jump up and down saying, "FOUL! HE

FOULED HIM! OH, WOW! DID YOU SEE THAT!" It won't matter whether or not a foul is called because someone is always fouling in basketball. You can always throw in a bunch of I-don't-believe-it-how-could-they-overlook-its and win the respect of every man in the room. Basketball, by the way, is the only sport where points are important. In the other majors it's the process.

Now baseball is called the American game and not for naught. It would take American ingenuity to come up with a sport that you do not have to be in good shape for, that takes all day, that you can get both mental and physical work done without interfering with your enjoyment of the contest. You simply must watch tennis and basketball to know what's going on. You need to see football replays so that you can talk about the tight end or nose tackle. It would help if you knew how the bowler was throwing in the first frame as compared to the ninth. A horse race isn't a race unless you are there when they say ". . . And they're off." But baseball . . . you can cook, clean, do your lawn work, read a book, play Scrabble, or pinochle. You can sleep, run errands, make love and still know what's going on. It's the perfect pastime because it demands nothing. The men who play it climb into their pajamas, wad up their mouths with tobacco or gum and stand around spitting all afternoon. Everybody can play baseball. If it wasn't such an institution I'm sure women would have tackled it way before they tried to break into the NBA or football or boxing. It makes far more sense for an all-female team to play against men in baseball than any other sport. Billie Jean and Martina played and defeated men in tennis, and though Bobby Riggs is old, tennis is not necessarily a game that yields to age. Bobby was not in that bad shape. But baseball? My home team has two of the oldest players in professional ball and the Cincinnati Reds are still making a run for it. Have you seen the bellies on those guys? If baseball doesn't work out for them they can always go to Japan and try sumo wrestling. Ladies, what I am suggesting is that you've been intimidated by sports and for no good reason. You've been cowered into being weekend widows because you think sweat is sacred.

Open that sports page, learn what a batting average is, pick a team, grab a beer and cheer. Just one PS here. Always take the underdog and points. Take the underdog even if you can't get points. I took the Dolphins over Chicago last year, and do you know that made me look like a genius? I was hot stuff. Always take the underdog, though, for another, more primordial reason. We're women. Somebody has to love the losers, too.

◆ ◆ ◆ ◆ ◆ ◆ ◆ ◆ ◆ ◆ ◆ ◆ ◆

A PATRIOTIC PLEA FOR POETRY JUSTICE
(Or Hey! Play the Game!)

Now that baseball season has ended, instead of being sad I'm mad. Not mad at baseball but the crap we have to go through to see a game. Baseball is already the world's most tranquil sport. It is probably the only active sport where you are not seriously required to be alive to play. Think about it. How would you really know, in the average game, if most of those players are alive? Oh sure, you're going to say because they spit; but do we really have any proof that a little spitting machine isn't installed in the position where the guy should be? Do we really know, except for the manager, that spit is coming from a human mouth? Now that a lot of the guys are blowing bubbles you can be sure a few of them are not human. I, for one, simply will not be convinced that Bill Buckner is any more than half human. I had a dollar, which in my conservative betting world is real money, on the Sox, and when Buckner went down for the last out in the sixth game, which would have clinched it for me and Boston, didn't I see a leg swing out at an odd and unnatural angle? I mean, if we can make a Stepford wife we can make a million-dollar ball player. Surely Ray Knight wasn't real. Here's a guy who hit every damned thing. That's unnatural, especially when you realize baseball is a game betting that you won't hit more than a third of the time. How can these things be explained? And poor Strawberry. Someone forgot his battery until the last game. Or as the announcer said, "When did he wake up?" I'm telling you a bunch of zombies and robots are out there. But that's not why I'm upset. I've had it up to my kister with "The Star-Spangled Banner."

OK. Let's start by admitting I'm a poet, and the purity of poetry is close to my heart. When Francis Scott Key wrote it, it was probably on the back of one of the envelopes Americans are famed for writing on. Key is out on a British ship watching the Stars and Stripes withstand one hell of a shelling. As dawn breaks he notices Old Glory is, tried but true, still standing. Hey, Key says to himself, this ought to be noted. Out whips the envelope, feather, penpoint, inkwell. "Oh, say, can you see . . .," starting one of the best-known poems in history. He finally is brought to shore and probably shows it to a friend, who immediately says, "You oughta take this thing to the Government. We need a good motto." I'm sure Key tried to explain it's not a motto, it's a poem. "We're Americans," his friend says, "we don't get into poetry. But hey! I know a good old English drinking song that if you change a line here and there it'll go to." Poor Key. There was probably some reluctance about changing his lines, but if it was good for the country . . . well, who is one poet to stand in the way? I mean, does anybody remember Robert Frost's poem for Jack Kennedy? And that happened in our lifetime! So Key's poem and the British drinking song were combined to make our national anthem. One reason it's so poorly sung, by the way, is you need to hoist a few before trying for those high notes, but that's definitely another discussion.

What irks me, as an American and a lover of baseball, is why do we have to hear it before each ball game? It's bad enough that we have to be introduced to the players. I mean, who really cares who's on the team? Are they going to play or what? If they're going to play, flash their position on the screen; if not, too damned bad. They just missed making the telly that day. If they want to be seen let them do something. But OK. I'm not being mean. Maybe we should let them be introduced. But honestly, I don't want it. I turn on the set, I want the game. I go to the ballpark, I want the first pitch. Not the ceremonial one; not the mayor; not someone who used to play ball in auk nine, but the guys who will actually do the game . . . that's all I want. We all know what time the game starts. If you can't get your beer and pizza before the appointed hour, too damned bad. You can always get it while the catcher is giving the pitcher his signs. But back to poor Francis Key.

He wrote a poem. I have no idea what is on Key's tombstone but it should read I WROTE A POEM. Have you actually sat through the concerts that are given before the game in the name of a poem? People start to sing "Oh, say, can you see" and in front of you literally lose their minds. They forget where they are and for what purpose they came. They begin to think that they are the show and try to make a statement. We should probably thank our lucky stars that Michael Jackson isn't a baseball fan or there would be no game at all that night as he moonwalks among the flashing lights hiccupping "OOOOOOOOSAYSAYSAY," with Paul McCartney and Stevie Wonder joining in. I could not believe Marvin Gaye the night he went on for five or six hours, only to be recently topped by Smokey Robinson, who combined *The Banner* with *The Beautiful.* This is baseball, not war. It was so much better when we the people sang it because somewhere around the second verse we would shout and scream for the game. You can even take it when the C & W people are called into action because they want a beer, but the rockers and the rhythm and blues people? Forget it. They want to make a statement. On a song that's unsingable. As if they didn't have concerts of their own. Let's see them have a bunch of ball players open for them. Yeah, that would be fair. Or, better yet, let's give *The Banner* back to the poets. Let's have it properly recited as Key conceived it. One person standing reading from one small envelope one little poem. Quickly. Concisely. With a sense of duty rather than feeling. I volunteer. Let's get those cards and letters going, campers, 'cause if we're not careful in the next year or two there won't be any time left for the game. Write your local newspaper and *USA Today*: Nikki—Quickly. *The Star-Spangled Banner.*

Or something like that.

◆ ◆ ◆ ◆ ◆ ◆ ◆ ◆ ◆ ◆ ◆ ◆ ◆

... AND
THE LOSER
IS ...

OK I've been pretty nice up until now. I have not actually by name called anyone a complete fool nor have I questioned the origins of their mothers' residence; yet it's got to be asked: Where do they get those sports announcers? Sure, the guys who write up the games are fools, too, but you don't have to read them. You can look at their dumb headlines and say, "I'm not going to read this fool today" and that's the end of that. But what can we do about announcers?

Tennis is the worst. I like tennis. In my younger days, and on one of my good, pain-free mornings I like to think if I didn't smoke, would work out and actually practice I could maybe have been a contender. I did join a spa and have been known to bench-press fifty pounds or so. I do three minutes on the LifeCycle and will, when all else fails, jog around the indoor track. I look good in athletic equipment. When I do the spa I, of course, have my shimmery tights on with contrasting color leg warmers. My towels are of imported cotton; I simply wouldn't be caught dead in a spa towel. I do my aerobics and, well, while I'm not in good shape I have clearly gotten no worse. I finish what I call a workout, sit in the steam, move over to the sauna, take a dip (as I cannot swim) in the pool, shower up and go home to watch tennis on cable. Sure it's all fantasy but it beats "adult" books and movies every time. I tune in and what do I hear? Bigotry. Pure and simple. A player is introduced: John Smith from Yugoslavia, number 114 in the world; last tournament the Cotton Grove, where he made semis. Then I have to see his earnings to date. Unfair. But mostly from then on he will be referred to as the Yugoslav, as if his damned name is too hard to pronounce. It's bad enough when it's Davis Cup, with country against country, but in individual play . . . unacceptable. They do it to the Swedes. As if Wilander, Edberg, Pernfors, Nystrom don't have names. They do it to the Czecho-slovakians to the point that *Sports Illustrated* had to finally say enough, no more Czech jokes. It's pathetic. Something in me cringes when I hear Hana Mandlikova called the Czech. I more or less expect Zina Garrison to be called the Nigger. Ninety percent of the commenting refers to the player's current home or the country in which he or she was born. When Noah won the French Open he became the Frenchman; when Hana recently beat Martina she was identified as "a soon-to-be Australian citizen." As if the crowd couldn't cheer for her because she's a great player. Becker carries all of West Germany on his shoulders, and it's some sort of national honor at stake when he plays Lendl, though of course the American announcers make a big deal out of cheering for Lendl since he (1) is a winner and (2) has a home in Connecticut. I have seen American crowds be downright ugly, and I can't help but think this is perpetuated by Bud Collins and company. Sports is supposed to be about the individual tuning his body to his highest effort then playing his best. But it turns into some sort of international substitute for balls. It's not fair to the athletes. Those of us who love tennis love it whether an American is in the tournament or not. John McEnroe didn't make tennis and he won't break it. He can only play for so long anyway. Yet their love of "Americans" rarely extends to showing Zina Garrison's or Lori McNeil's tournaments. The biases are pathetic. You can actually tune in a tennis match and listen to the announcers and never know there's a sports contest going on. We have to hear about and see the players' friends, their coaches, parents, everything but the match. Wimbledon is the best called because the British usually do it and they do the tennis. There is no other sport in which the players' origins play such a big part.

In football the teams are introduced and the players' college and hometown are listed. Then on with the game. In basketball the same. In both those sports the history of the player may come up as in "The Raiders traded him last year and here he is sacking the quarterback," but that's it. In basketball the same trading history is given and that's it. You would never hear an announcer say the Georgian or the North Carolinian or the Californian just upended the nose tackle or the white boy dunked the ball. The last time there was a racist remark on the air in football ("Look at that little monkey run") an immediate apology was issued, and it's not been done since. Yet tennis, the most international of all major sports, suffers from what can be called zenophobia at best and at worse —racism. It needs to be stopped. It's ruining our game and making no converts.

Why are announcers dumb? Maybe they were born that way. Maybe the fact that most of them used to want to think they had some sort of ability makes them so narrow-minded. The great players like O.J. Simpson and Bill Russell are great announcers because they know and love the game. And stick to the game in the comments. O.J. was the best football commentator on television. He predicted the right man and the right plays to watch, then you could sit back and watch what he said unfold. Bring back O.J. Bill Russell is great because he knows what is going on on the floor. Oscar Robertson was a great commentator, but the coaches didn't like him because he pointed out their mistakes. Bring back the Big O. We want people out there who will help us see what's going on; who love what they do. And who will stick to the game on the floor, not the one they wished had been. I saw Virginia play Villanova recently and all they could talk about was Polynice. Well, what about the five guys on the floor who didn't steal, who studied, who trained hard to play the game? And the bad thing is, Virginia was winning. All we could hear about was how they couldn't go to the final four without a dominating center. It's the scourge of American reporting. What is actually happening is not the news. The news seems to be what *will* happen. All those men sitting there with their mikes up close to their lips want to be fortune-tellers. They want to predict. Well, a sports contest isn't a place to predict. Just call the game. Keep track of the fouls, the yards, the score. Try not to miss the opening kickoff and try not to cut the game off before the clock goes to zero. Is that too much to ask? Apparently. Grow up, sports announcers. We really don't care about your old games and what you did and didn't do. If we cared we would tune in "Great Moments in Sports" from the Old Guys. We want the game at hand. We want a fair, impartial call. Speaking of which, when are we going to pay the refs? From what I've seen recently those guys have to be on some kind of take. The worst calls get made, then stand. OK. It's only human to make a mistake. But the instant replay was made for mistakes. That should be an official time out. Or at least something sensible, like the guy who asks for the replay, if he's wrong, will lose a time out. It's not fair to have a better method of judging, then punish the people who use it. If the defense thinks the offense fouled, then the defense asks for a replay. If the offense did not foul, then the defense loses a time out. You'd have to be pretty sure before you wasted a time out challenging a call. We have got to do something because I cheer for the underdog a lot and it seems most bad calls go against the perceived loser. But all refs in all sports need better pay. Tennis especially. It's too hard calling a six-figure game on a three-figure salary. Just as baseball has its All-Star Game tennis should have some sort of tournament to pay salaries/benefits for the refs. At least the players and their fans could feel things were more professional and less emotional. I also have to say it: We need more Blacks and women in the announcers' booths. We need nonplayers, too. Most people watching a game never played the sport. The nonplayers look at things differently. I know I love a good effort.

I am also a hometown nut. I like the Reds, the Bengals, the University of Cincinnati. I don't mind when we don't win so much as I mind when we don't seem to try. But a losing team becomes the butt of all those old, out-of-shape guys sitting there. I like a try-try-again mentality. And sometimes the home crowd could use a dose of compassion. In other words, guys, it's only a game. A game that pays a lot of money and a game that makes a lot of money, but to those of us on the other side of the tube it's fun, it's a hip hip hooray. It's a way of cheering for something. Don't keep taking away from the effort on the field nor the effort in front of the TV screen. We just want to cheer. Since most teams are losers, as there is only one number one player, only one Super Bowl championship team, only one World Series winner, most teams and most fans have identified at one time or another with a loser. That's life. Most of us lose, too. And it's not the worst thing in the world to say "Well done." At a certain level of excellence we are all the winners. And maybe the guys in the booth ought to think about that. Or maybe the women in the booth will be sure to mention it in the wrap-up.

SACRED COWS . . . AND OTHER EDIBLES

◆ ◆ ◆ ◆ ◆ ◆ ◆ ◆ ◆ ◆ ◆ ◆ ◆

SACRED COWS . . .
AND OTHER
EDIBLES

Well, OK, it seems to always fall on me to tell the truth and, hey, I don't mind. It's not nearly as bad a job as some people think. First of all, saying what you actually think energizes your mind for more creative solutions; not to mention freeing you from remembering what you once said and now have to backtrack on. It also allows you to offend everyone right away so that there are no false notions on either part. Now I'm not so truthful that if a, say, slightly overweight friend buys a dress with lots and lots of stripes going round and round I'll be the one to say, "God! You look just awful!" No. I am not cruel. Neither am I the sort of person who, visiting a friend with flu or something, will say, "Je-sus! You look like you're at death's door." I have been known to eat rubbery omelets that friends have made, exclaiming positively between munches at their unique texture; not to mention loving, absolutely lapping up every tender morsel my son ever cooked. I have, after all, been properly reared. But neighbors, I have to say it because no one else will. The rich have more fun than we do. I know that flies in the face of accepted wisdom. I know that there is an entire school of intellectualism which spends its time and energy trying to tell poor people how much better off we are than those with means. And I'm not talking about the working rich; I mean the filthy rich. The working rich, of course, have jobs that they have to go to every day. No. It's the filthy rich who come in for pity. People sit in their little, hot, about-the-size-of-a-decent-closet unair-conditioned apartments and pontificate thusly: "I wouldn't want all that money. It don't seem to make them happy." And folks, that's a lie. The rich are happy out of their fucking minds because they don't have to be in the hot, sweaty city sitting on their behinds contemplating the problems of the poor. They are not inconvenienced by store clerks who are insulting, traffic cops who stop them for seat belt violations, citizens who feel their one task in life is stopping you from smoking in public places. They don't have to worry with laundromats that take their quarters then refuse to dry the clothes; they don't get the nasty letters computers write asking, "DID YOU FORGET US LAST MONTH? . . ." Cars that break down with the very thing that just fell out of warranty; furniture that breaks before the second payment; children who tear their new clothes before church on Sunday—the shit in life that drives you crazy. The filthy rich don't have to worry about their health because they can afford doctors and surgery, but before they get to that they can afford proper shelter, good food; recreation . . . things that make life fun and worth living. They rarely have to worry about their sex lives, either, since everybody wants to screw them and they don't have to pay the pregnancy price since they can afford abortions whether they are legal or not. There's a conspiracy out there against us, the working poor. We are, as the sign says: Overtaxed, Underpaid, Not Appreciated At All. And we are expected to feel good about our situation because, after all, we could be worse off. Hey, we could be better off, too, but we are not encouraged to think that way. Sacred cows make hamburger meat just like the rest of them. We are being turned away from the very thing we need: a healthy dose of selfishness.

Now greed, as anyone will tell you, is a terrible thing. I know; I look at *Wheel of Fortune, Let's Make a Deal,* a couple of those shows almost every day and see people at lust for just one more spin, spin on things any fool should know. I saw one woman who hit the third-round $5,000 space two times, netting her almost $80,000 when she had:

The Th--ll of ---tory

The --ony of defe-t

The woman gave that smile of the terminally dull and said, "I guess I'll have to spin again." She hit bankrupt. My mother said the woman did not know the answer and I suppose if that's true she truly did not deserve to win. Yet how could she not know? Education is free in the United States. Compulsory, actually. Did she graduate from one of our fine Christian academies which did not want to burden her mind with quotations from anything other than the Great Book? Did she sit, her junior year in high school, dreaming of a White Christmas? I mean, how could she not know? But then, I have seen Monty Hall give people $1,000 cold cash and watched them trade it away for Curtain Three: two dead goats and a banana peel. *Let's Make a Deal* is the second all-time cheapest show on television. Anytime you get cash you should take it and sit tight for The Big Deal. I know, you are wondering what is the all-time cheapest? I must confess I do not often look at it because it upsets my stomach: *The All-New Newlywed Game*. The last time I actually sat through it the question was: "Name your husband's favorite fowl." And none of the three wives could say chicken, duck, quail, squab, turkey, capon, Cornish or guinea hen. I'm talking not even Sally Rand, folks. Nothing with feathers at all. Which is only comparable in my mind to the wife who, I hasten to add, is no more stupid than her husband, answered "Potato chips" when asked her husband's favorite condiment. We're probably lucky she didn't say, "We're not using birth control." And what makes these three couples expose their absolute stupidity five times a week? Why, the desire for "A prize picked especially for you," which frequently turns out to be an all new no-stick ice cube tray. "Yes, Dave and Sue, *The All-New Newlywed Game* has picked out for you your very own ice cube trays in shocking pink. You can fill these trays with water for the next two hundred years without fear of leakage. And what do we have for the runner-up, Merle?" Or is Merle on another show? That's greed. Though not greed for money but greed for fame. Can't you see those people going back to Someplace, Pennsylvania, asking their friends did they watch the show? Many a young couple has probably gone into debt for a VCR just so they could tape and maintain their appearance. That show, neighbors, is grounds for divorce. "What do you mean I'm so hot the water in the bed boiled?" (while hitting him with the cardboard answer sheet). "Oh, honey, you were all over me . . ." (while smiling sweetly because he knows we know nobody in his entire life was ever all over him for any rhyme or reason). Selfishness can be a terrible thing but I'm talking healthy selfishness . . . enlightened self-interest . . . let's call it "controlled ambition." Sure, a lot of people still prefer blame to responsibilities; excuses to explanations; desires to decisions. And that's pitiful. But let's face it, guys. We've got to start somewhere.

I've decided I'm sick of poverty. Sure, I know I'm not as bad off as some but, neighbors, let's be honest—I'm a hell of a whole lot worse than others. I see those *kids* running around in that little Mercedes-Benz that the last time I priced it was going for $60,000. Before you get the wrong impression let me explain why I was even on the Benz lot in the first place.

My mother purchased a Cadillac. A big, black Seville that did everything but make your morning coffee for you. My mother has always wanted a Cadillac. As you probably already know my mother is colored and it's not really that a Cadillac is a colored person's dream but, well, dammit, my mother wanted a Cadillac. It seemed a small enough thing to want after working at schoolteaching for five years at $100 a month, then working for the county for another twenty-six years or so at not a whole lot better. She and my father had sent two girls (my sister and me) to college, had purchased a nice but rather plain home in Lincoln Heights, and she just never did want a lot of stuff. Our furniture is comfortable but old: Mom dresses expensively but she never wears anything out and hasn't gained weight since my birth. It just seemed like a little thing to ask for ... a Cadillac. When she started talking new car, which Lord in heaven knew she needed, I wanted her to look at the Peugeot, which is what I drove. It's not all that much, but it's nice and it looks good. Eventually she agreed and bought one. Everything was fine. She said she had purchased her last car as she was considering retirement and all she wanted to do was pay for it and quit working. Now, I don't know what you know about the French, and maybe I'm even bordering on some level of lawsuit, but the French are a strange people. They're moody. They make arbitrary decisions based on things like their pride or something. They also made a car that nobody can service but their own people. You can't even use a normal wrench to let the oil out for an oil change. No matter. We had the Peugeot dealer less than two miles from our home—until he started to sell the Datson. The French didn't want him to sell the Datsun, or so we were told, and one thing leading to another as is wont to happen then bingo! He no longer sold or serviced the Peugeot. Not to matter: We found a foreign car place that had one man who could service the car—until he decided he was needed in Israel and went back home. Winter came and I probably don't even need to tell you the rest. Winters in Ohio are cold ... very cold ... freezing. Her car froze. Triple A could not get it started. Nobody could get it started. I called the hot line number for car service and was told my nearest dealer was in Dayton or Lexington. You've probably seen the ad for the Washington wine that has the French people sitting around at a taste test. They all just love that wine. It's great. "Where," one of the men asks, "does this wine come from?" He and another man walk over to a globe and the host says, "Washington," pointing to Washington State on the globe. "It appears to be a suburb of California." Of course, you and I would laugh; at least I laughed because the idea of Washington being a suburb of California is funny. But neither Dayton nor Lexington is a suburb of Cincinnati, either. How the hell was I suppose' to get a car that is not running to a dealer fifty miles north of me or one hundred miles south?

The car had to go. And may the moody French never sell another to someone's unsuspecting mother again.

I have a theory about parents. Treat them like adults and they will respond. That's not always true of parents and grown children, which is one reason most parents and grown children cannot live together. Both want to treat each other as if they were children. Plus, folks, I had made a hell of a blunder recommending my car. My car worked because I had lived in New York City where it had had proper maintenance. I drove back to Manhattan enough to have it serviced on that end and hadn't realized the implications of owning a car that was not constantly on the road. I was, quite honestly, thankful that Mom never said to me, "I wouldn't be in this mess if it hadn't been for you." I don't think of myself as guilt-ridden but I do feel bad when things I recommend don't work out. I wisely decided to ask what she wanted in a car. "Well, Hortense and Willie have a Mercedes-Benz," she said. "Would you like to go look at one?" I asked. So we did. You know you're in trouble with the Benz when you walk on the lot and see the repairmen in jackets. Somebody has to pay for those clean hands. But hey. If you can't afford it you shouldn't be looking. I, in fact, have a friend who says the reason she drives a Mercedes is that she's poor and can't afford to replace cars either regularly or often. Makes sense to me. We took a test drive. The people couldn't have been any nicer. Then Mom asked how much. Mommy is by no means cheap. Frugal yes, but not cheap. She just was having the hardest time seeing a car that cost about twice what her home did sitting out front. No Sedan for her, no 190 either. "Well, maybe I'm interested in something smaller," she says, "like that one." She had pointed to the 450SL. I turned my head; the salesman perked up. He almost picked her up to carry her to it. That "little car" carried a price tag that said "$60,000." Mommy couldn't believe it. "For that little thing," she kept saying as I slowly, with as much dignity as I could manage, walked her back to the old car. She still hasn't really recovered. Even now she'll see one on the road and exclaim that that little car cost so much. I gave her space, then a couple of weeks later asked if she was still interested. "I want a Cadillac," she had decided. "Fine by me," I cheerfully agreed, and we went Cadillac shopping. There was really no question but that it was love at first sight. That 1980 Seville is one of the most beautiful cars ever designed. It's sleek, it's sexy, its lights turn on by themselves at dusk; if you have a heavy friend in the back, "level ride" will pump in to keep the car even. The sound system is great. You name it, the car has it.

She purchased a diesel. Mistake. For the first hundred miles or so everything was fine, then for no reason the car would die on you. I had it one day going to town and it died on the expressway. Folks, that's a lot of car to go dead on you in the inside lane. The final straw was when we went to the World's Fair in Knoxville. The Seville died in Lexington and I had to rent a Toyota to get us there. Ninety percent of owning a Cadillac is to show it off to your friends. Knoxville is my mother's hometown. If that car wasn't going to take her to Knoxville then she didn't need it. We pulled up in this Toyota. The next day I drove back to Lexington to pick up the Seville. It wasn't fixed. I drove back to Knoxville. The next morning I was scheduled to open the fair for Knoxville College Day. We are now into Sunday so I know Monday morning the car will be ready. I leave my mother and my son and his friend and drive back up to Lexington. I have by this time gotten to know the good folks of Raccoon Valley very well. We are friends. I stop in for gas and the lady is saying, "Still having trouble with your car?" I have made friends with the Wendy's people in Lexington where I get my coffee. "Car still not ready?" they ask, then whisper to each other. People all up and down that road see me going north and south and shake their heads. I can read the trucker's lips: "That poor woman's car ain't done yet, Jeb." And they blow their horns at me and give me the high sign. My mother did not become a Cadillac owner to have her youngest daughter become an object of pity. We do finally get back to Cincinnati and I immediately go get *Car and Driver* or *Road Worthy* or some book to tell me what the best car on the road is . . . Toyota! What is the purpose of a car? To get you where you want to go. How does it do that? You stick the key in and it starts. What are the side purposes? None. Fuck prestige. Fuck looking good. Fuck a friend that needs to see you in a hunk of steel that fucks up. I only in life, dear Lord, want a car that will run. But how to convince Mother?

One thing was becoming clear to me—I could not take this. I hate a moody car more than I hate a moody man. At least the slump of his shoulders or the scowl on his face will tell you when trouble is coming. With a car you never know. And like an unfaithful mate, once a car has let you down you never sort of trust it again. How to convince Mother? I called my sister. There are, I deeply feel, advantages to being an only child. I have an only child and would not change that for all the tea in China. But neither would I give anything for my sister. I guess Gary and I are lucky because we are not only kin, not only do we like each other, but we bring different skills to our relationship. I can easily whip Mom in shape by saying, "I'll have to call Gary on this." Its not that Mom is afraid of Gary but Gary takes no prisoners. The minute her mind is set on something it's got to go her way. Knowing how Mommy felt about the Seville I knew I needed more than a threat; I needed a body. "Can you come home?" I whined pitifully over the wire. "I need help." Gary, true to her giving nature, said, "I'll be right there. What's the matter?" I felt foolish. "We need to get rid of the Cadillac and Mommy loves it and I can't tell her what to do." "I'll tell her," Gary cheerfully volunteered; "get her on the phone." "No no. That can't be the strategy this time. You be on her side and let me insist. It'll be better if she's mad at me than you." "Whatever." When Gary got home a couple of days later she started praising the car and I knocked it. After two days of that Gary says to me, "Well if you hate it so much trade it." "Mom likes it," I reply as Mom is sitting there watching us go at each other. "Well if you knew what you were doing she wouldn't be having these problems," Gary says. "Mommy, why don't you come to California with me? Nikki doesn't know what she's doing."

Mommy, I think it's fair to say, is fond of me. She also knows I would do anything to make her happy. I guess it's fair to say I'm fond of her. Gary starts insisting that we keep the car despite a "little aggravation." "If you come with me I'll keep your car running." Mommy has begun to panic. She doesn't want me to look bad in front of Gary. She still sees us as her ultracompetent older daughter and the nontalented, bad-skinned younger. She needs to protect me. Gary laid it on about how Mommy was right; I took one hell of a thrashing. Then the maternal instincts began to win out. "Well, I don't like that car all that much," she opines. "I've been thinking about trading it." Gary went into violent no's! "You love that car. Don't let her make you trade it." It was a masterful performance. Mommy insisted that she wanted to. By that evening we owned a beautiful white Toyota. Mommy for sure was upset with me because she never cared for that car all through summer and fall. But that first winter we had three or four days of zero weather. Our next-door neighbor's new Chevrolet froze; our across-the-street neighbor's brand new Chrysler corporation car froze. Hell! Triple A couldn't start one morning. But we did. "I really didn't like that car when I bought it," Mommy said, "but now I see why you wanted me to have it." "I? I had nothing to do with it." "Oh fiddlesticks," she said. "I saw through that dog and pony show you and Gary were running when you started." There is a moral to this story. In case you missed it I think I should explain: When you are poor nothing works right. I don't care if it's the top of the line or the bottom of the heap; it won't work right. Also, it is very difficult to fool your mother. I advise against it.

Being Black and poor is, I think, radically different from being anything else and poor. Poor, to most Blacks, is a state of mind. Those who accept it are poor; those who struggle are middle class. One of the saddest things that has happened to the Black community lately is that young people have begun describing their neighborhoods as "ghettos." We never thought of ourselves as living in a ghetto though very clearly we did. Another is that our young people are believing that white people control the world, that they have no control over their lives. When I was growing up if you flunked out of school, got pregnant, stayed drunk all the time, you were simply "no good." You had let your family and The Race down. Now you do that and worse and you are a victim. It's no surprise our communities are going to hell in a hand basket; Black leadership has finally managed to convince the young that it's neither their fault nor their responsibility. It wouldn't surprise me one bit if we ran a poll and discovered people *really* think if they change their hairstyle or toothpaste or deodorant that they will live happily ever after. The level of fantasy, unreality, is absurd. In the good old days when people finally got something, they knew it was well deserved, overpaid for and wouldn't last anyway. Today we have scores of youngsters, young men mostly, who are totally unable to accept success. There's something terribly wrong with being the number one draft choice of the defending NBA Championship team, then snorting cocaine and dying; there's something terribly sad about a bachelor party turning into death camp; there's something downright tacky about having several Superbowl rings, then pushing drugs to buy your son a birthday present. Why can't these kids enjoy their successes? Because the current crop of what passes for leadership has said to them over and over again white people control your destiny and exploit you. Young men who get a chance to go to college on athletic scholarships feel exploited and demand more. Not more education, but more things. And find that they are still tacky thugs who sexually abuse women and still cannot read a book. Though it is agreed it is exploitation to put them on an academic track and, dammit, unfair to expect them to perform off-court as well as they do on-court. Young women who have an opportunity to participate in beauty pagents and model and all those silly girly things that a few years ago would have been unavailable are made to feel that they are being taken. Why? Because they believe in magical transformations. They believe they should be "happy" simply because they have used what few gifts they have. What is that old Moms Mabley joke: ". . . you are still a Negro . . . you were on your way to Cleveland but you fooled around with that Indian and missed your bus." I guess my age is showing but I remember when seeing *any* Black face on television was an event. People would call around the country, "There's a Black girl on *The Sixty-Four Thousand Dollar Question*," and we'd stop whatever we were doing and cheer for her. Despite its stupidity, whenever I need a quick Black fix I can tune in *The All-New Newlywed Game* because they always have a Black couple. Yes, making the same Black fools of themselves, but there, nonetheless. And why not? It's America and the whole country makes fools of ourselves. If America had style we'd never have come this far. Black leadership is tacky. And I guess that's American, too, but it's boring. Somebody needs to say to all of us: BEING GROWN IS NO DAMNED FUN. The Urban League's bumper sticker (which I don't have the slightest notion if they even do bumper stickers) should say LIFE SUCKS, 'cause it's true. But we live it nonetheless and hopefully find some fulfillment and a teeny tiny bit of happiness. The problems of the Black community are no different from any other communities: We work too hard; get paid too little; and nobody gives a damn. But that's no reason to give up and blame anyone else. That's the real world. If we could come through indenturement, chattel, emancipation, Black laws, segregation and just plain we-don't-like-your-kind-isms, we can come through "exploitation" that pays little boys millions of dollars to play games and pageants that pay little girls to walk around in swimsuits. But hey, I've strayed. Poor is a state of mind.

To state the obvious is not necessarily to agree with it. There's always some smart ass out there who'll say, "If poor is a state of mind then we should change our minds," then proceed to extol the virtues of some mind-altering drug. No. No. No. I'm even a bit beyond "Just Say No" into say "HELL NO." Drugs are death. No. If poor is a state of mind it must be embraced. James Baldwin, in one of his most beautiful sentences, says, "You must embrace what you fear." Makes sense. Again, age is probably a factor. When I was growing up nobody had cars. Everybody walked. The boys developed walks, took walking to a fine art. They dipped and swayed. You had no trouble telling what was going on by how they walked down the street. One walk for going to see the girls; another for getting together with the guys; a third for going to work; another for coming home. It was street ballet at its highest. Which certainly beats the whining we see today ... which is infinitely better than the drooped shoulders and dragging spirits we encounter on the streets today. Black men used to walk with a "look at me" walk. Now they seem to walk within a shadow. They don't want to be seen and that's not good. When the men don't strut the women don't smile; and property values go down because nobody cares. The NAACP's new campaign should be "STRUT!" Aimed at young men. It should point out the significance of education, good health, responsibility. But why do I go on about leadership? I already know they don't talk to us; they don't live with us; their children don't go to school with ours; they don't work a real job. How could they know what's going on in the projects, communities, rural areas of the country? They are "national leaders," and if we have suffered from a spate of false issues, well that's obviously too damned bad. So what if every poll taken shows that Black leadership and Black people differ considerably on the issues? They are not so much leading us as they are making white people feel bad about our condition. And if those conditions have not and cannot improve with this leadership posture, well, that's too bad, too. If they changed they'd have to admit that we, the Black people who comprise the Black communities, are free. And a free people choose their representatives and spokespeople; a free people take joy in their responsibilities and experience sorrow at their failures; a free people set goals and map strategies to obtain them. A free people are, quite simply, free. And would therefore need no one to beg for us.

OK. I didn't really mean to get on Black leadership, but now that I did ... I am fascinated. There seem to be two common denominators to leadership of color: They hang on until they are carried away in a casket; and they don't believe in any dissent. To disagree with "established" leadership is considered by those self-same gentlemen treason. This, despite the fact that they are supposed to be speaking for us. It would be laughable if it weren't so sad. They will accuse Reagan (the President) of not listening to them but they don't listen to anyone. The purpose of any leadership is to build more leadership. The purpose of being a spokesman is to speak until the people gain a voice. I am totally convinced the saddest thing that happened to Black leadership was the Civil Rights Act of 1964. If the people have civil rights then the next task is to exercise them. How do a people exercise civil rights? Individually. We have got to be the only community on earth that wants our people to do better but not the individuals who comprise our people. If that makes sense to you you are either a Black leader or I have a bridge I'd like to talk to you about. It makes no sense at all. Our people have fought a long, difficult battle for the right to be seen as individuals, and what do we find in 1986? Quotas that say we need so many bodies of such and such hues; so many male, so many female. It's no wonder no one takes pride in his work. He's not working; his color is. It's no wonder young people don't think they need to study for school; it's all going to be quotaed out anyway. Individual effort has been sapped, and we as a nation continue to pay for the lack of joy in individual achievement. Life is not a national lottery where chance controls the die. I'll say it again: LIFE SUCKS, but its all we have and we ought to be joyful about the responsibilities we shoulder. Katharine Hepburn once said (if I may paraphrase), "Life is rough; it kills you." It doesn't just single out Black people for death; it doesn't just kill white people. It kills everyone. We don't need terrorists to take us hostage; we are all hostage; we don't need murderers to kill us, life will do that. Rich or poor; male or female; the proud and the profane alike. The Good Book teaches us, "Man born of woman will die" and if the prophets had been a bit more daring a couple of thousand years ago they would also have pointed out man conceived in a test tube will die. If you are on this earth you cannot get off alive. Fact. Fancy: Can you make something of your life? That's the question. Can you turn off the people who deliberately use you for their own limited ends to make some sense, gain some joy, love somebody? Can you wake up in the morning with someplace to go and come back in the evening to somebody who cares? Unemployment must surely be the worst thing on earth. To know that you are not needed for anything, not even a menial sweeping the streets or stacking bricks or anything at all. Benefits can't take the place of work. Benefits are necessary to smooth the transistion but we need jobs. There is no such thing as "make-work" because all work is made by somebody. All work is necessary. I don't have any trouble seeing why people become abusive when they don't work. They feel useless. And all the social work in the world will not make them feel better. They need a job to go to or be studying for. People need a purpose. I know I do. I know I would feel different if I had nothing to do all day. Even if I hit the Ohio Lottery (and I sincerely hope I do) I'll find something to do with my time. Maybe I'll be able to structure my week instead of my day. I'll know that I need to be at the library to read for the Children's Hour on Tuesdays instead of in the classroom at 8:30 A.M. on Monday; I'll maybe, even be able to say in March I take my annual cruise instead of at 7:30 P.M. I watch *Jeopardy*, but it will still be an ordered life. I'll get to pencil shopping trips in the fall instead of when my dogs go to the vet; skiing trips at Christmas instead of reminders to get sidewalk salt. Hell yes, I would be rich and love it. No confusion here at all. No whining from me about how money has made me terribly unhappy. I can handle it! But I've deviated. It's got to be the most emotionally devastating thing to know you are not needed. It's not right. Whether it's make-work or make 'em work, people need something to do to contribute to the common good. When you think about the cave people, as I frequently do lately, what is absolutely striking is that someone, probably a woman, drew a figure on a wall. Why would she do that? To make her cave more beautiful? To say to future dwellers that humans were here? To communicate something within her soul? Why would she do that if it weren't important to her? To see the plains dwellers fashioning, in the dwindling light, a figure on a bowl . . . why would she do that? Why would primitive humans, despite all the dangers they faced, want to create something? I have to think it's because we all want to do what is expected of us and then a little more. Could we really be so different from our plains-dwelling–cave-dwelling ancestors? We all want to do our share and then some of us want to make it beautiful. Yet I remain puzzled.

Why don't Black people ever want to relinquish the reins of leadership? Why don't they have enough faith in us to step aside and allow new, local leadership to emerge? Why do we in the Black world mostly have to vote with a gun and not a ballot to make changes? Aside from the Communist/Capitalist wars of attrition, why haven't we built an infrastructure, a generation after colonialism ended, that gives us a score of leaders to draw upon? We have one man who probably at the beginning was very good and then he dies or gets killed and we get another man and, in the words of Stephen Bishop, ". . . on and on . . ." Whether it's the president of a country or the mayor of a city or a city councilman, you can bet your bottom dollar they will hang on and . . . God bless them . . . someone in the Black community five years after their deaths will still be voting for them. It's no wonder we stagnate, we have the same old tired ideas circulating through the same old tired leaders until finally there is nothing left to defend but the idea of leadership itself. Sort of like Nixon in blackface. "Don't criticize me because that's an attack on the presidency." Great Foolishness. "Don't criticize Black leadership because that's an attack on Black people." What does that sign say? WE THE WILLING, LEAD BY THE UNKNOWING ARE DOING THE INPOSSIBLE . . . WE HAVE DONE SO MUCH FOR SO LONG WITH SO LITTLE WE ARE NOW QUALIFIED TO DO ANYTHING WITH NOTHING. It's the credo of Black people. Did I leave out the part about gratitude? Try being Black and doing something extraordinary and you'll learn pronto what ingratitude is. You are simply not allowed to be Black and happy about your success. It's taken as a sign of spite by Black leadership. No one ever wants to talk about how well we have done, especially under the circumstances. We always need to show our scars. We the willing led by the unknowing always have to apologize if we do well. It's the unwritten code of Blacks and, if I may, women. You are never to say "I DID IT." You are always to say how many people you have left behind and how if they had had your "breaks" they, too, would excel. Folks, a lot of people wouldn't excel if you gave them Heaven on tuna fish. They'd eat the damned thing. A lot of people, let's be honest, can't even answer a damned telephone the way you want it answered. They don't come to work on time and don't work once they get there. They have a shit-eating attitude and should their supervisor mention that to them they write him up with the personnel office on discrimination. A lot of people that you would want to network with and share little company secrets with will go to the company picnic and drink too much and say you said your supervisor is dumb. A lot of others will go to the Christmas party with their spouse, who then proceeds to discuss how despicable white people are and how its spouse is being exploited. A lot will not be able to write a decent memo and will charge they are being held back because of gender or race. And others will not go on out of town trips then be angry because they can't get promoted. But hey, you caught my drift. I just believe we are the masters of our fate. We may not get all we deserve but I don't know who does. At any rate . . . It's still tough being poor. It's still tough to look at the catalogues and know you can't order. It's still unfair that some have an awful lot and others have nothing. I just think it's a good thing to take control of your ambition.

Having shared all that, let me say I'm easy. It's true. I learned a long time ago, maybe before I even knew that I was learning it, to be happy with what I have. Not content as in I-deserve-this-bullshit but rather since-this-is-mine-I-may-as-well-make-it-what-I-want-it-to-be. No matter how rich I would have become, if I would have been rich I would not own a big house. My idea of both luxury and security is the top floor of the best hotel in town. I'd adore being rich enough to live in the Beverly Wilshire or the

Plaza or the Georges V or any Continental or Hyatt. I want someplace to sleep, another area to sit, a bathroom and, of course, room
service. It's not that I don't cook; I do. And I'm a very good cook.
It's just so boring to wake up in the morning having to decide
what, rather than where, to eat tonight. I only eat once a day and
it depresses me to think about food the first thing. I really can't
imagine how people manage who have to think of breakfast and
lunch too. And you wonder why housewives drink. I don't. At the
risk of a feminist picket line running around bookstores that stock
this book, the hardest job in the world is the work women who
stay at home do. This work can never be adequately compensated
for by money, though money would help. Women's work is the
pits because it's a limited audience for a show that plays every day
seven days a week. Women who leave home have it made. They
can easily explain their irritability by blaming it on the job; we
who stay home have to rely on the premenstrual syndrome. Women
who leave home can explain dull dinners and no breakfast or lunch
at all by saying, "But I'm working so hard to give you things you
need." We who stay home picking up smelly socks, making up
tousled beds, cleaning dishes, dusting furniture, planting flowers
nobody sees . . . we're just so much garbage giving both our children and husbands, not to mention dogs, cats or other pets, a false
notion of our worth. There is nothing so undervalued as women's
work. I'm probably as guilty as the next working woman in not
understanding my sister mothers who stay home. Until my father
became ill I lived in Manhattan, had a housekeeper, went to work
every morning and returned to a clean home and occasionally
dinner in the evening. I must say I made my own bed and counted
my own laundry but I never thought much about the work of a
house. When my father had a stroke I moved back to my parents'
home. All of a sudden I found myself with time on my hands
waiting for him to need something. The house itself is old and
needed work. I began to work on it. Before we venture further let
me say I know I should have bought a new house. It would have
been, in the long run, cheaper and easier. But Gus didn't want to

move and Mommy didn't want to move so that left bringing our home up to our standards.

Gus, my father, had obviously been sicker longer than we had noticed. We noticed when he was felled with a stroke but we probably should have noticed when little things that he used to do weren't getting done. I guess when you're married to someone for over forty years you don't want to notice things because that reminds you that both of you are getting old. That is probably poorly said but what I mean is I think it's hard to admit how much people change. Anyway, we had a slow leak in the bathroom, which had buckled the floor. Mommy said she didn't notice it; Gus was in the hospital so he could say nothing. The easiest thing to do was put another floor in. The problem is finding workmen. I never knew what my grandmother meant when she said, "You got to beg 'em and pay 'em too." About a month back home I found myself using that expression a lot. We got the new floor put in, though; I was totally pleased. Mommy said it looked nice. This is not about putting the floor in. Once you do a really big inside job everyone says it looks nice. This is about waxing the floor. I would wax the floor and no one would notice. We put in an oak kitchen floor next. Everyone said how great it looked. I would Murphy that floor and no one would notice. No one notices now and the floor is six or seven years old. Mommy does. I do when she Murphy's it. It got me thinking. I would dust the furniture then feed it with lemon oil. That furniture would shine, glow, come alive. My friends would say, "Your house always looks nice." Maybe so. No maybe, definitely. But Your-house-always-looks-nice does not respond to my inner need to have people exclaim over my work. I want each wood piece delicately examined and lovingly commented upon. I want each piece of crystal to be observed for the way the light bends through it; I want, dammit, the silver that sits out to be individually praised. If my glass was spotted and dull, if my floor was greasy and dirty, if my silver had yellow stains it would be noticed. But if you keep a clean house it's an "Oh, well. We expect that of you." It's not fair. When I get on my hands and knees to put Murphy's oil on that floor I want it noticed. And nobody does. I quickly understood that woman's work is noticed only on its absence. Even women who should know better will ignore your effort. If a man does any little thing at work, let alone anything extra, everybody goes to Hosannahs. But a women is expected to do these things with no praise and in fact no notice taken. She will only hear about it if it's not done. No one says "Great dinner, dear." But you can bet your bottom dollar they'll all scream "What! Meat loaf again?" No one says "I love the new way you made up the bed." But you can count on criticism— "Marge, why isn't this bed made up?"—when he comes home. No wonder housewives are skittish. They get nothing but negative feedback. I have taken to observing and commenting positively on any change that occurs in any friend or relative's house. I try to see how things are and what they are trying to do with it. I always like it because (1) it's not my house and (2) I don't have to live in it. I expect the same uncritical support. If we stay-at-homes are not supportive of each other all is lost. I also remind my working-out-of-the-home friends that the reason we stay-at-homes have better-looking houses is we have nothing better to do with our time. Otherwise we women are playing a vicious one-upmanship game with each other; both trying to prove we are right in a situation that is neither right nor wrong; just different. Sacred cows make very poor gladiators.

Wait. Let's pursue that for a moment longer. There are two totally illogical things that people, more specifically women, do: (1) have children and (2) try to make homes. These are two thankless tasks and should be undertaken with extreme caution. I have friends, I'll be honest about it, who think I am good with children. I probably am because I do not treat them as children but as people. It always scares the bejesus out of me to hear a parent speak of "the baby" as if the child had no name, no personality, no individuality. Many people speak more personally of their dogs or cats than they do their children. You sometimes wonder why they have bothered to have children at all. Or you get that what

I really think is sick situation where some parent drones on about how the child is his or her best friend. I never trust that. We go through entirely too much to have children to end up with only a best friend. Even though I do have a best friend I know there is a world of difference between her and my child. For one thing I'm not responsible for my best friend's bills. For another, though I rejoice when things go well, and am quite sad when things don't . . . I know it's neither my personal triumph over street thugs and indifference nor is it sad enough to make me question my values in life. Children aren't friends . . . they're joyful responsibilities. But it's illogical nonetheless that something that happened, in many cases quite by accident, and as a side product of something else entirely, can change your life. Just another little reminder that things do not always work out as we think. I don't so much like children as I like my child. There are reasons for this: (1) he's mine and I've paid for him; (2) he's a nice young man and (3) I know that no matter how this relationship ultimately works out I do not, nor does anyone else, own him. There wasn't a whole lot I was looking for in a child. I just wanted basic intelligence, some sensitivity and a hell of a whole lot of sense of self. I figured if I taught him not to take my shit I would have given him about all a parent can give a child. That will, I admit, occasionally cause problems with his algebra teacher or the vice principal but hey! He doesn't have to be perfect, just the best he can be. Houses, on the other hand, are freely chosen after much thought, many evaluations and every possible consideration. I'm sure there is the perfect house somewhere. I read *House and Garden, Architectural Digest, Home* among other things and I see perfect houses. I just don't know anyone who lives in one. I don't know anyone who ever has. And even when I look at those gorgeous mansions, lovely Manhattan pied-à-terres, charming little caves in Utah or somewhere I say to myself, "I'll bet that basement leaks," or "They probably have a termite problem," or "God! What their heating bill must be." It's not that I have the best house, it's simply the reality that there is no better. Like children . . . or cars. No matter what you get someone gets something better and someone gets something worse. The whole trick to life is the simple recognition that "No option makes the best choice," followed by some variation of "But he's our rascal." STRUT. It's all we have left.

I have a sad tale to tell. It's not about my house because in reality I don't have a house; I live in my mother and father's house, but as long as I'm coming through the door I may as well wipe my feet. We're smokers, my mother and I. My father was a smoker when he was alive; my sister is a smoker. I don't mention this as any sort of pride in bad habits but as a reality. Some people don't smoke because they don't like to. Some don't smoke because they were too old to learn by the time it became available. And a few assholes don't smoke because they think it's just the cutest thing in life to say, "I doesn't smoke. Please put out your cigarette." Or something of that nature. Nonsmokers have gone way over the brink about clean air. A more reasonable worry would be that the water we drink and the air in the streets is tainted by leaks and accidents of our industrial society. Of course they also think industry should be shut down, and what they'd really like is one day to wake up in a forest with nothing and no one on earth but them and Bambi. Hell, cave people didn't smoke; plains dwellers didn't smoke; Neanderthal man didn't smoke, to name a few of our ancestors of the last million years or so, and they lived about fifteen or twenty years. Not that anyone has to put up with my smoke; they don't. You just have no right to require me to stop. Prohibition was stupid in the twenties and it's stupid now. It's not really the nonsmokers who really tear my curtains, it's the ex-smokers. Nothing on earth is as righteous as a reformed prostitute. Little old ladies who hated their husbands for forty years of marriage wait until he dies, then get on the bandwagon. The only thing I know that makes me half as angry is to see a man walking a picket line against abortion. Especially a Black man. To see those hypocrites who could not honestly tell you their own children are well fed and well clothed—"well" here to mean fed and clothed at all—saying to some woman they neither know nor want to know that she has to use her body twice in the service of mankind: first to screw him; next to have his baby. It drives you nuts. To see white people talking against abortion when there is not one Black man, woman or child whose life and right to life they respect. What do they want us to do? Have babies so that the ghetto can continue? Do they warehouse children in their spare time? I mean, why the hell can't, couldn't a woman and in many, many cases, a girl choose not to have a baby? I won't even argue whether or not an embryo is a child; I think since it is in the female's body she is the one who should make the decision about bringing it out. Any man who doesn't like it can easily prevent his sperm from fertilizing her egg by any number of methods, first among which is abstinence. "JUST SAY NO" should be aimed at men the women are so obviously going around seducing. Very few guys are taken against their will; very few women run out of gas on dark roads; I mean when was the last time you saw a television show with some female stalking some guy in the dark and pulling him down in some alley? Give me a break. Abortion is about women having options and anti-abortion is about men taking them away. Hester Prynne should not have worn her "A" alone; there were two parties involved. But then I never believed Eve seduced Adam. It's illogical. I also reject the idea that sex is punishment. Psych 101 teaches us if you put two people, no matter what their race, religion, ideology, of the opposite sex in a room . . . sex will happen. We further learn from Kinsey to Masters and Johnson that if you put two people, no matter what their race, religion ideology, of the same sex in the same room . . . sex will happen. But further we know if you leave one person, no matter what race, religion ideology, etc., in a room alone . . . sex will happen. The rat, in other words, will cross the grail more for sex than for food. We ought to stop this foolishness of controlling or trying to control sexual behavior and be supportive of people's control over their own lives. But we were talking smoking. Sorry. Since we all smoke our walls have to be painted every five years or so. I would imagine that even folks who do not smoke get their walls painted but I have never seen data on this. My mother and I live in a small house. I like to think of it as a cottage. If we were surrounded by a couple of acres we could put Heidi to shame. I like that old house. It's illogical, but I do. We had discussed having the house painted but like a lot of old ladies who live together we have accumulated a lot of things over the years ... tiny little things like the elephants my mother collects and the hippopotami that I do. It's amazing how many elephants you can get once you are in a place for thirty years or so. I also collect Black memorabilia so there are a million little Black figurines. Not to mention little photographs of everybody, every occasion and everything. We are now, quite honestly, in a position to bring nothing into the house unless we are willing to take something out. I suppose there will always be room for one more family photo but I swear it's getting close. It's even becoming a pleasure to shop again because there is no possibility of purchasing anything. The standing Christmas rule for the last five years is: A gift may not be given if it's not consumable, usable (as in perfumes, lotions or soaps) or won't die soon (as in cut flowers). Painting is, and ever will be at my home, a pain in the ass. Mother kept hinting that perhaps the gook on the walls needed to be painted and since I would do anything to avoid the painters I would get my Big Wally or whatever that stuff is and ask, "Where? Where is there a spot?" That was working fine until the day my mother's bed broke. And this is the sad part. My mother's bed broke.

My mother is a small woman, four feet eleven inches, not weighing quite one hundred pounds. I wouldn't say mother is undemanding because in her own way she is; yet she's not overbearing, and dammit, the bed broke. I was sitting reading in my favorite rocker with the game going when she brought it up: "My bed broke," in a very sweet, gentle voice. Well, nobody should have to sleep on a broken bed. How long had they had it anyway? There aren't too many things in life people are absolutely, unqualifiedly, unquestionably entitled to, and a bed is certainly one. She could not have picked a better time to have a bed breakdown than when she did because Shilito's was having a bed sale. Not to worry, I assured her. As soon as the game is over we will go to Tri-County and buy a bed. It was fall, the leaves were changing, yet not really cold. I put on my boots, she dressed as little old ladies are prone to dress for special occasions and we headed out to get a bed.

Sometimes when you wear boots that squeak and jeans that are, well, gamy, a sweatshirt that has seen a better day or two, salesclerks will ignore you. Even if you are with your mother who looks every ounce a lady. Not today. A very cheerful woman came practically running over to us. While she did not actually break into a sweat she was a bit winded as she asked to help us. I don't like to fool around; I hate pretending I don't care when I'm shopping. I like to tell them what I want and have them go get it. I have friends who say you will get a better deal if you feign indifference but I don't want a better deal; I want what I came for: "We need a double bed for my mother. Today. To be delivered on Monday." That put it square in the salesclerk's court. We look, finally deciding upon a cherry bed that was, really, quite lovely. "It doesn't go with my chest of drawers," Mommy whispered as the sale was being written up. "Hey. We need a chest of drawers," I said. Politely. But pointedly. It's sometimes necessary to spread a little guilt around since in fact we hadn't been asked about the chest of drawers. "Do you think," this little voice comes up at me, "I need a night table, too?" Now I'm really not a bad shopper. I prefer to antique if I'm going to do furniture but I really didn't care. What I wanted was happiness and to get back in time for the second game. Plus, honestly, I thought she really deserved and needed this bed so what could the big deal be? "Mother, get a bedroom suite. Please." My mother is a frugal woman. She needs you to persuade her to spend her own money. Even if it had been my money I would not have cared because, dammit, she needed a bed. "You deserve this, Mother. And it's beautiful. Should we get a new lamp? Rugs? I really do want you to have it all." She only wanted a double bed, chest of drawers and a night table. To be delivered on Monday. We went home happy. Now this is a sad story so how could we be happy? Because we were dumb . . . stupid even . . . definitely foolish if we thought anything could be that easy. How could it be that girl and mother purchase bed; bed is delivered; girl and mother are happy. No. Girl and mother are of color. Nothing could be so simple.

Sunday morning in an unbelievable, yes, even unnaturally good mood I arose, fed the dogs, started my coffee, stripped the ads from the Sunday paper, poured my coffee, then settled with my comics. I always read Miss Manners last figuring, rightfully so, that the Forum section (Week In Review for you *New York Times* fans) will depress me. She's right, you know. If simple courtesy were practiced more, if we were less inclined as a species to be boorish, selfish, vengeful, we'd be better off. MISS MANNERS FOR PRESIDENT. I don't read the *NYT* anymore since migrating Midwest. For one thing I don't care and for the *all* important *other* there is no comic page. I had subscribed to *USA Today* thinking they would eventually recognize the need for comics. I mean, really now . . . what's a paper without comics? How can you really begin the day without knowing what Opus is doing? Some people just expect too much of us—so I settled into my largely reduced paper to read my comics first, sports page next, Forum, arts & leisure, Lifestyle and wrap it up with the magazine gossip section (Didn't Dipsy Doodle, gorgeous star of *To Hell with You*, used to have a mole on her right cheek? I say yes but my husband says no. If he is right I have to perform an unnatural act on him. Worried, Standby, Missouri. Keep that tongue in cheek, Worried. Dipsy, noted for turning those quick phrases, did indeed have a mole on her cheek. She got rid of it when Vanna White made the cover of *Time*. "Who wants to be different these days when there's a fortune to be made?" Do *you* have a question about the stars? Write us. We have the answers.) Yes. Actually I am ashamed of reading things like that, but hey, who wants to be left out? You never know when something will come up in conversation. I had a young militant tell me recently that he disliked Magic Johnson because his (Johnson's) wife is white. There are reasons, I suppose, if you deal with that sort of thing, to dislike Magic Johnson. As a dyed-in-the-wool Celtics fan, though I wish Mr. Johnson no harm, his playing ability disturbs me. But because of his wife? I was proud to very sweetly say, since I read gossip, that "Mr. Johnson has no wife. He are single." Usually you may have noted when people have prejudices and you have information you have to repeat the information several times before they get it through their thick skulls that they are forming opinions on false information. "Well, his girlfriend is white." Now my son tells me I have become everybody's mother and that is probably true also but it pains me to hear hatred and stupidity coming out of young Black mouths. "Well, I want to thank you, young man, because I just learned something. I was under the obviously false impression that I watched Magic Johnson play basketball. I didn't realize tuning into the Lakers was some sort of validation of Magic's choice of companions." "Well I still don't like him" was the reply. "And neither he nor I give a shit" was mine. I gotta tell you this. He was a nice kid. After I got to know him better I understood his problem; he wants the Race to do better. By the way, I have no idea in 1987 who Magic Johnson dates, nor, at forty-three, do I care. I'm long out of the running. Plus, I like short men.

So Mommy gets up and I say, as we have a game at 1:00 P.M., "Let's clear your room out now." Monday I have to go to work and I don't want them coming to deliver the bed and chest of drawers and night table and be unable to since the union will not allow them to help a sixty-plus-year-old woman move her furniture. By getting the stuff out on Sunday, though, Mommy will have to sleep in the den. Not to worry. It is only for one night.

There is nothing so small as an empty room . . . nor so dirty. The walls looked like shit. A very quiet voice suggested—at third and long—that perhaps the room needed painting. At third and long you would say yes to a tour of hell in a beaver coat. What I really remember is the "Oh, goody" from the other side of the table and me trying to figure out why she was as happy as I that my team had made first down.

OK. So I hadn't wanted to have the house painted, but one room, which was empty now—how much trouble could that be? Monday I called to delay the delivery and she called a painter. He'd be there tomorrow. "You got to beg 'em and pay 'em too." Tuesday came and went. Our next delivery was Thursday. Wednesday came and went. Call to delay delivery. By Friday I have decided to paint the damned room myself.

Painting isn't hard. You purchase paint, paintbrushes, get a ladder and put the paint on. Mostly. Almost. Sort of? I miscalculated the amount of paint I'd need. No one told me you need semi-gloss. Flat looks like shit. And paint splatters. In your hair, on your clothes but mostly, neighbors, over your floor. And it will not easily come up. By this time I have to admit it. I am annoyed. It's been a week—the house is torn up and the paint job I did was not good. Mommy, having some idea of my limits, knew it was time to call somebody. Frankly, friends, as I look back on it all, I was about one aggravation from burning the house down. Tennessee Williams has always been one of my favorite writers, though *Streetcar* is not my favorite play, but in one blinding flash I understood Stanley. Of course you flip the dishes onto the floor when asked to help. You are at the end of your rope. Mommy's friend, Hortense, who already got Mom into the bind over the Benz, has a daughter who just married a very big (as in important) rock star and they were redecorating their condo and Van just loves her decorator. We finally snare him. "Why," he asks, "are you painting one room? Why the whole house will only cost you——" and he named a not cheap but not unreasonable figure. All righty. But I would have said yes to anything by now. As we stood there in the kitchen, someone, I can't really recall who, said, "The kitchen sure could use some new wallpaper and maybe a little tile over there where we fry all the time." Yes. And just one other minor point. Very minor. I had not noticed until Theresa had a stroke that our steps are high. For example, where the average sane person's home would have two steps, we had one. You can actually huff and puff coming up that step. The steps leading to the patio were in the same condition. Theresa Elliott is a dear friend to us and a great barbecuer. After her stroke she had to go out the side door through the garage to get to the patio to barbecue. I had called a contracter to put new steps in. He was delighted to do the work but he couldn't do it in the summer— he was busy. But by October first he would be there. October one, with her room empty and badly painted, the house torn up, the wallpaperer working . . . Skip sent his men. Without asking, having, in fact, no knowledge of the distress going on inside, they started that machine that tears up concrete. My patio steps to the house, my steps to the garage were all gone. I understood completely Scarlett O'Hara: NEVER AGAIN WILL MY FAMILY GO THROUGH THIS.

OK. It's time to fess up. I wasn't always able to be calm in the face of disaster. I used to, in fact, during my early college years, kick back with a beer or two. Then I got busy and just plain didn't like the taste of alcohol anyway and hey, I hadn't had a drink in maybe fifteen, sixteen years. I needed a drink. I'm teaching my writing class at the Mount and every morning my students look worriedly at me—How's the house coming? And I would share the latest. When I walked in that Monday, now into my third week of this mess, to say, "I have no back steps at all," uncontrollable weeping broke out. A wave of Oh my God's could be heard breaking over the back of the room. Women started beating their breasts—How much more can she take, Sweet Jesus? Even my younger students who have never known the sorrows of home ownership fought back tears. Is there anything we can do? Poor Linda, upon hearing of the steps and herself contemplating renovation in her own house; poor Linda who had already dissolved into pants and oversized sweaters from the neat little lawyer suits she always wore; poor Linda whose hair, generally tied into a neat little bun, which at the beginning of this saga was coal black, turned gray. To this day, dear friend that she is, she doesn't admit that my class did it. But I know. I was there. I then recognized there was only one way to get on top of this thing. I had to pretend, from that moment on, that it was not happening.

My world turned a hazy red—either sunrise or sunset—I was not sure and did not especially want to know. My two dogs, Wendy and Bruno, were being forced to defecate in the basement, which was beneath their dignity. I actually saw our Thanksgiving pheasant being cooked in my den on an open fire—the ceiling which Bobby and I had so carefully laid turning black from the smoke. I understood for the first time in my life why people cease trying—why folks give up, why we who are poor think there is no end to our troubles. How could something as simple as a bed lead me this low? Once before, with this house, I had been so tested. Once before I had seen on my floor little droppings that I knew had come from something eating at my foundation; once before I had been given more than I thought I could handle. We had termites.

Now really, I am aware of the food chain. I am, in fact, a strong supporter of the darter snail. I believe everything has a right to exist, should, in fact, be secure in its integrity, but neighbors—I hate an insect. They have not created the insect whose death does not bring rejoicing to me. I have been known, among my son's friends, to offer a bounty for the body of a wasp. Even now if they need a few pennies for gasoline I'm perfectly willing, for the body of a waterbug, to part with five bucks. Even the little bees that buzz my flowers can only escape my Raid for a brief period. Nothing will stop me in getting to kill a fly. I, in fact, hate them so much I do preventive spraying. I thought, and until I noticed that sort of powdery substance on my floor, that I hated flies the worst. But then I discovered termites.

First of all, what I actually hate about insects aside from them being ugly, crunchy, sneaky little teeny tiny sons of bitches is they are un-American. They're Commies. "Yeah, sure," you're saying, "ants are flag-carrying, Marxist-reading, Mao-suited Reds. Yuk. Yuk." But hey, look here. They are organized in cells, there is a hierarchy of work divided along the lines of what's good for the group; there is no possibility of changing your future or job through individual effort; and if you go away from your group you will perish. There is no thinking on your own, no innovation, nothing to mark that you were here and had a dream. They work so well because they keep doing the same thing over and over again. Those of the human species who think that neat, who say things like we ought to be united and each one do a prespecified job are looking to insects for leadership. And who in her right mind would want to be a drone? The humans advocating droneship intend, in fact, to be the queens anyway. They are advocating droneship for the rest of us. If I have to choose I much prefer the mustang free on the plain or the thoroughbred running a race ... the lone wolf howling on the hill; the coyote still seeking a way to exist on the prairie. Not a fucking termite. Under any circumstances.

I'm told by my Terminix man that you cannot hear termites. They silently eat your house away. But I swear I can hear the little buggers digesting my wood and shitting it out. I hear them in my wall laughing at me. I hear them sliding toward my bookcase deciding they will take my favorite volumes. Forget the Stephen Kings, the Sidney Sheldons, the Jacqueline Susanns and Jackie Collinses. They want my Toni Morrisons, my James Cleveland records right below her, my dictionaries, my maps ... my whole fucking life. I called the exterminator. "Oh," he says, "not a bad problem at all. We can handle it." But once you have been leered at you fear rape. "How do I know they won't come back?" "We can tent your house and nothing will come back. Everything will be dead." Actually it sounded good to me. "Everything?" "Yeah. Bees, wasps, ants, crickets—all the pests." Now wait, I don't want to appear to be vacillating, but crickets? I grew up with "Brownie and the Cook." It's not only bad luck to kill a cricket but honestly, how can you say Jiminy Cricket is a pest? Crickets sing and dance and don't hurt anybody. Willfully harming a cricket is right up there with clubbing baby seals. But those g.d. termites have got to go.

When everything deteriorates time changes; your life rolls slowly,

slowly before you. You see your errors, you once again bitter-sweetly touch the sweet parts. You see yourself unable to make changes. Words, that have the power to change things, spew from your mouth only to be trapped in bubbles slowed down by molasses. The world goes in slow motion. How long have we been working on this house? Was it really November and my tile is still not complete? Would the bed, chest of drawers and night table ever get in? Would the concrete set? Would Wendy ever, ever forgive me for the indignities she suffered? One bright, though chilly morning, they all left. The quiet, like fog on the Ohio River, folded over the house. We were clean, tiled, painted, wallpapered, concreted, railed. I could not believe it. Broke but happy, my heart turned to Thanksgiving while my finger dialed Shilito's. This is called DON'T THEY EVER LEARN? Yes, neighbors. There is more horror coming our way. But first, let's take a commercial break.

I discovered something a few yeas ago. You cannot be (1) sane; (2) a female; and (3) look at daytime television. You can only do two of those things at the same time. From the 6:30 A.M. shows until 8:00 A.M. it is considered that the men are at home. That something, in fact, serious, can happen. You get your real news (THE WORLD WAS BLOWN UP AT 1:35 A.M. EST. EVERYBODY DIED.) You get your real people (THE PRESIDENT OF THE UNITED STATES AND ALL THE LEADERSHIP OF CONGRESS WILL BOTH BE WITH DAVID THIS MORNING . . .) You are, in other words, treated as a sensible adult. At 8:01 A.M. this all comes to a halt: *Screeeeech*!! And the attack begins. "Hate that gray? Wash it away." You haven't even combed your hair this morning let alone contemplated its color and texture. But wait, what have we here? "Some people call these 'age spots' . . . but I call them UGLY!" This is delivered to us by a little old lady in a house neat as a pin who clearly has been married for the last fifty years. Are we really to think he would leave her because of liver spots? Then well be gone. He should have split years ago, giving her a chance to find someone who valued her for more than her body. But if that doesn't drive you to drink, how about the woman sitting in front of the mirror talking to God knows whom saying, "John felt old when he saw the gray in my hair." Give me a break. John *is* old. And the color of your hair will not change his physical condition. She, of course, uses some product that not only keeps her marriage intact but the son of a bitch actually takes her out dancing! I hope she finds a better man. But now we see the morning mist in the background. A powerful car, its motor purring, is coming into view. Are we women finally to get a real ad? In the right-hand corner creeps the picture of a little cottage. If it weren't so obviously European we would say "shack." "Françoise! Françoise!" shouts the overjoyed woman in the seed sack dress with children pouring, like clowns from a circus car, out around her feet. "How do you manage to look so young?" Not hello. Not how are you? Françoise so obviously is rich that a more appropriate question would be when did you get your latest face-lift? Plus this poor simpleton, concerned about fading youth, is probably an abused wife. Anybody with all those children surely will qualify. Françoise not only is driving a great car, she probably is a single woman with an exciting career. She has probably spent the night with "Roger," who is pressuring her to make a commitment. Whenever she feels herself weakening she drives out to see this poor soul; be renewed in her commitment never to marry and returns to Paris quite content with her life. Porcelana indeed. Common fucking sense is more like it. But hey, if I was a guy I would resent some of these pitches obviously aimed at keeping woman in "her place." There is this ungrateful dummy who climbs into the shower with the water running. We could maybe overlook it if there was no water because maybe he didn't realize that little room with no windows and a spigot hanging down was the shower. But no. The water is running. After wetting himself he leans out of the shower calling, "Hon, get me a towel." No "please." Not even her name. She stops what she is doing, wiping her hands on her apron, and brings him a towel. Does he look sheepish for having forgotten it in the first place? Does he smile in gratitude at her bringing it? He sniffs. "Are you sure this towel is clean?" The answer to which is, "Are you wet or what?" This pitiful excuse for a human being is probably in middle management. He probably makes important economic decisions affecting thousands of lives—but he can't remember to get his own towel and is not appreciative when helped out. And that's supposed to induce me to buy fabric softener? I'd sooner shake myself. The world, of course, is incensed by Ring Around the Collar. Doesn't he wash his neck? Doesn't he know that if his hair is clean this won't be a problem? But, hey, it's no wonder housewives are crazy. By 8:30 A.M. your entire being has come under assault. Noting with guilt that you do, in fact, have yellow waxy buildup; looking with disgust upon your gray hair and wrinkles, you do what most people do. You stare at your hands. "DO YOU HAVE ROUGH, RED HANDS?" they boom at you. They do seem to always have these things perfectly timed. "THEN YOU NEED PALMOLIVE DISHWASHING LIQUID." I swear, one day somebody is going to kill Madge. Madge sitting there reaping a living off the misery of other people. Madge with the big mouth and smart-ass saying about hands. Hands that have washed diapers and floors. Hands that do dishes three and occasionally four times a day. Hands that have to wipe up dog shit and pick the paper out of the yard. Hands that haul cases of beer home so that his weekend will go smoothly. Madge is putting down these hands! Someone ought to lay reality on Madge and point out what her hands were like before she agreed to bear his children and keep his house clean; before she agreed to wash and iron his shirts in a washer that never breaks down with an iron that won't burn. These are not friends to women since there is never a break. The vacuum is not a friend to woman since our floors are supposed to be free of all signs that life has passed in this room. The dearest friend of woman in the home is the microwave, which frees her from watching the same sacred cow unthaw, cook and brown. We will be entirely free, sisters, when we see the ad with Bernard standing there: "Sure, I use the forty-eight–hour girdle. When Cathy met me my stomach was flat. I owe it to her to look good." Or Steven. "Hi. I just want to talk to the men. When Myrtle and I met I knew it was my hair that attracted her to me. So now I use Mr. Robin's Wigs. They look just like real hair. And when we go out no one says, 'Who's that old guy you're out with?' " We will know equality has sneaked in when Edward says, "I washed dishes. And I tried them all. No liquid could do what a servant can. I bought Ann a full-time maid. After all . . . we deserve the best." Of course, someone is asking about the maid's hands. Well, how about a dishwasher? If she's Black she'll whip that household into shape, toote sweet. And hey, we can't all be winners.

The bed was arriving in the morning.

I know how Charlie Brown feels in the fall. He is standing there, hopeful . . . pitifully so . . . waiting to kick the football Lucy is holding for him. He knows, because he has been through it before, that she will snap it away just as he reaches it. But he wants to believe. I, too, wanted to believe the bed would arrive. And it did.

Cherrywood double bed, chest of drawers, nightstand. Beautiful. Put the chest of drawers here; the nightstand there; the bed in between. No. We ordered a double bed. I measured it myself. Yes, I do know how to read measurements. I, after all, successfully completed fifth grade. THIS IS NOT A DOUBLE BED. What do you mean beds come in one size to be double or queen!! If we had wanted a "queen size" bed we would have purchased and paid for it. Get this piece of crap out of my house! What does that mean: You don't take back, you just deliver. Calm down! CALM DOWN? C A L M D O W N ???

Clearly I was on the verge of hyperventilating. I went into my newly painted, wallpapered and tiled kitchen. Calm down, I started saying to myself. You knew it couldn't go smoothly. You are, after all, still colored. There are times when religion plays a big part. The only thing between me and a fatal heart attack was Job. I contemplated the rather horrible example God made of Job while showing off for the Devil. "Consider my servant Job." And I could see how a similar conversation could take place: "Consider my servant Nikki." And the Devil replying, "Well, certainly. Look at what you've done for her." Not that my life has been easy or anything—I think I could raise a tear or two for me. But on the whole, I'm alive, relatively sane, earn a living off my insanities, have a loving family, faithful dogs, a house that is, right now, quite beautiful, a car that mostly runs and good credit. Perhaps I haven't reached high enough but on the whole . . . it could be a lot worse. I thought, as I sat smoking, about my fellow humans going through the daily hassles and it occurred to me . . . I should do something. I should start the Society of Job. At first I thought to restrict membership to Black women, then I thought, "Naw." Sensitive Black men have the same kind of hassles. So, yeah, let's offer some comfort to the men. Then I thought of White, Brown, Red, Yellow women who were hassled by things out of their control. Then, of course, I simply had to consider White, Brown, Red, Yellow men. Should membership be restricted to the English-speaking? Of course not. And if not restricted to the English-speaking then how could we ignore the anguish of female elephants who watch their mates be murdered for tusks or young rhinoceri who watch their fathers, gentle males, vegetarians who would only attack to protect their families be shot down because of a superstition that their horns make human men screw better; how could we ignore the fears of female seals that their babies would once again be clubbed to death for their fur or the worry of all whales that they will be assassinated for perfume factories? I finally understood we are already a part of the Society of Job. It's only a question of who will force themselves away from our comfort by insisting upon their right to commit murder, rape, genocide, ignorance, indifference. I felt better.

I dismantled the bed and hauled it out to our garage. I wrote the president of the store a very nice letter detailing our affection for his company and a desire to have his very fine merchandise removed FROM MY GARAGE. I said lovingly, gently, though, I confess, with great firmness, to my mother, "Should you ever again in this life mention a bed to me I will have you committed. I do have grounds, Mother," I continued, "since only a clearly crazy person would ever in this life mention a bed to me again."

And what have I learned? The rich do indeed have more fun than you and I. I do believe it would have been just as difficult if I were rich but I would have been able to hire someone to be aggravated. I know, honestly, that I'm a better person for having handled everything myself for I learned to question everything. Nothing is easy; nothing is sacred. Somehow, you and I, the ordinary grunts who get up in the morning, go to work, make a little less than we owe, come home at night to a house that needs a little more than we are willing to do, to people we are periodically not sure we should be bothered with and on the contrary not at all sure we deserve, and we will lay down at night on our own mattress and box springs mounted on the little legs we purchased from our hardware store, say our prayers to a God we are not sure is listening and close our eyes to the howling of sacred cows on their way to the slaughterhouse. We may not know the truth but we've learned to question the suspect. And after all, neighbors, isn't that a beginning? Knowing we'll have fresh hamburgers in the morning?

. . . FILM
AT
ELEVEN

◆ ◆ ◆ ◆ ◆ ◆ ◆ ◆ ◆ ◆ ◆ ◆ ◆

OUR OWN HOUSE
IS IN
DISORDER

The Civil Rights train, in 1965, pulled into the station for rest and refurbishing. It had been mightily battered but was still on track with Martin Luther King, Jr. conducting though his fireman, Malcolm X, had been, for reasons still unclear, shot down. Three years later the train was not so much derailed as diverted by the assassination of King. It was reassigned first to the Peace Movement, then to the Woman's Movement where it did honorable though still unfinished work. It has not yet returned to the inner city.

Our old are on the streets, sleeping in parks, being forcibily moved into prison-shelters (where a refusal to accept "help" is taken as prima facie evidence of insanity), standing in what has become the longest food line since the Great Depression, unable to make food stamps, welfare, Social Security stretch from the first to the thirtieth.

Our young are out of school, out of work, out of hope; unable to read effectively or write with clarity; imprisoned by self-hatred and institutional racism they prey, like the walking wounded they are, on the old, on the helpless, on themselves.

The New York Police Department tortured five suspects with

electric prods; shot a sixty-six-year-old grandmother to death on an eviction . . . and there was no outcry.

A Los Angeles policeman murdered a seven-year-old boy because he was home alone watching television while his mother went out at night to work . . . and there were no sanctions.

The Philadelphia Police Department bombed a Black neighborhood, then a few months later that same city had to declare a State of Emergency because a Black couple moved into (and out of) a "white" area. And there are no marches.

Our Black college student population was reduced by a bit over 10 percent last year, as were the numbers of Blacks entering professional schools: doctors to heal us; lawyers to fight for our rights; teachers to educate us; future leaders to help us shape the twenty-first century. Our own house is in serious disorder.

Twenty years after the Voting Rights Act, twenty-one years after the Civil Rights Act, thirty-one years after *Brown* we are still separate and unequal. It is, I believe, good and proper to help others, yet I recall a line from the old Thanksgiving hymn: "Sing Praises to His name—He forgets not His own."

♦ ♦ ♦ ♦ ♦ ♦ ♦ ♦ ♦ ♦ ♦ ♦ ♦

PIONEERS:
A VIEW
OF HOME

I don't own a class ring. Actually, I didn't graduate from high school, but that's not the reason I don't own a class ring. I was an "early entrant" to Fisk University but I am sure that, had I asked, Austin High in Knoxville would have let me purchase a high school class ring. It wasn't the lack of money, either. My grandmother, who simply adored any kind of ceremony, would have been as happy as a pig in you know what if I had wanted to come back to Knoxville to receive some sort of something with my class . . . and purchase a class ring in the process. Nor did I forget. Proms and class rings aren't the sort of things you forget when you're sixteen or seventeen years old. No. It just seemed foolish. What do you do with a class ring after you are graduated? Give it to a girl if you are a boy, but if you are a girl . . . maybe pass it along to your daughter? I know one mother who did that. Put it in your jewelry box? I know lots of people who did that. Lose it? Certainly. God knows it's a sign of a really sick mind to see grown people, adults with responsibilities, wearing class rings. I go so far as to submit you know a person is having a severe personality crisis if you see a high school class ring on a finger beyond the first semester in college. Male or female. It's a big sign saying NOTHING HAS MATTERED TO MY LIFE SINCE SENIOR YEAR.

I don't own a yearbook from college, either. I did pay my fees and really could have sworn that a yearbook was included but none ever arrived. A friend of mine recently went to live in Indonesia and left a copy of her yearbook with me. She thought, quite correctly, that I would want the book with the photo of me sleeping in the Honors Lounge. No one can tell it's me, though I happen to recognize the desert boots, but aside from those and a beige skirt that I actually hated, no one would know it's me. Still and all I admit pride that I made the yearbook one year. Maybe another year, too, but no one has stepped forward with another copy. I'm not against pride. Not at all. I'm just a little picky about what I take pride in.

There are actually people who take pride in their race. This is actually stupid. You would think, the way some people act, that there is a Babyland somewhere in which babies could select their parents: "I'll take the rich, white ones." "Well, I want the Black ones." "WHO'LL TAKE THE POOR? WE NEED MORE POOR HERE." "Oh, hell. I'll take them. You been yelling for that poor family for over a week!" "WHAT ABOUT AMERICANS? WHO WANTS TO BE AN AMERICAN?" "I want to live in Nepal. Got any Nepalese who want children soon?" No. I rather doubt that it happens that way. More likely two people happened to meet, mated, and you were born. Not that anyone should be ashamed of his race, it's just that when you think about it you had nothing to do with it. Not your race, nor your age, nor your nationality. Not even your name, though some of us sneak and vary our names more to our liking somewhere between the fifth grade and college—with which I sympathize. No one wants to be called "Snookums" or "Boo-bee" through eternity. It's a question of style.

I was watching *Family Feud* recently on our rerun station. Some of you remember *Family Feud*: Two families squared off with really silly questions answered by the strangest one hundred people in the world ("We asked one hundred people to name a friendly neighborhood bird") and the families had to guess what these fabled one hundred had said ("Buzzards"), and whichever reached 350 points first ("The number one answer—27 points") then got the chance to name national products for $10,000. A Black family consisting of, if memory serves me correctly, a father, mother, two daughters and a son-in-law was playing a white family consisting of a father, mother and three sons in uniforms. As luck would have it, on the third round, where all values are tripled, the Black family answered and got to play for the big money. Richard Dawson went over to shake the hands of the white folks and thank them for coming. You remember that you win the money in front of you (*Family Feud* wasn't a cheap show like *Jeopardy*, where only the winners get to keep the money), and Dawson pointed that out and said he was sorry they didn't do any better. You understand, Dawson wasn't expressing regret, just being polite, when one of the sons piped up with, "Well, we still can fly." I guess they were in the Air Force, but mostly that was such a racist remark. You Blacks may know what one hundred people think but hey, we whites can fly. Totally unnecessary. And tacky. I don't object to the boys being proud of flying; hey, if I could fly I'd be proud too. As a matter of fact I'm proud of myself when I *board* a flight! I'd be snuff in a pitcher's jaw if I could actually make that thing leave the ground. No. It was the context in which the remark was made. As if, "Well, hell, after all we're still white" could make up for the fact that they lost. That's as bad as if the Black family had whipped out the old Red, Black and Green nationalist flag and proclaimed superiority for Blacks based on . . . *Family Feud?* In the words of Joan Rivers: "Oh, puhleeeaase."

It's so clear, now that we have photographs from the moon, and man-made satellites even farther away, that earth resembles nothing so much as a single cell in the human body. That's not my observation; it belongs to the biologist Lewis Thomas. I was never good at biology. You stood around in a room with lots of little dead animals in jars and you were expected to cut them up and discover things. Or you started with live worms or frogs and you killed them to discover twitching muscles and stuff. I don't deny the importance of Life under the microscope or scalpel . . . I just don't do it. But what a concept. That the planet upon which we live is no more than a specimen on a slide. We, who think humans are nature's greatest invention, may well turn out to be no more than the life we see swimming in an ordinary drop of water. What then is important? When Paul Tsongas, the former senator from Massachussetts, was told he had some form of cancer, he decided to quit the Senate. "No one ever died saying, 'I should have spent more time at the office,' " he pointed out. No one ever died saying I should have hated more; I should have had more guilt or envy in my heart; I should have beaten my wife; I should have been less educated; I should have stifled my personal urge to explore my world and my life more. No. Most of us face our fading years wishing we had been more open, more loving, more capable.

They say Home . . . is where when you go . . . they have to take you in. I rather prefer Home . . . when you could go anywhere . . . is the place you prefer to be. I don't think of a home as a house, which is another thing I don't own. Certainly, though, I do live in a house that I have made my home. I won't even pretend living on the streets, sleeping in public parks, washing up at the bus or train station, eating out of garbage cans is a valid alternative to bedrooms, bathrooms and kitchens whiffing good smells every time the furnace blows. But I also readily concede if there is no love a building will not compensate. The true joy, perhaps, of being a Black American is that we really have no home. Europeans bought us; but the Africans sold. If we are to be human we must forgive both . . . or neither. It has become acceptable, in the last decade or so, for intellectuals to concede Black Americans did not come here of our own volition; yet, I submit that just as slavery took away our choice so also did the overcrowded, disease-ridden cities of Europe; so also did religious persecution; so also did the abject and all but unspeakable Inquisition of the Spanish; so also did starvation in Italy; so also did the black, rotten potatoes lying in the fields of Ireland. No one came to the New World in a cruise ship. They all came because they had to. They were poor, hungry, criminal, persecuted individuals who would rather chance dropping off the ends of the earth than stay inert knowing both their body and spirit were slowly having the life squeezed from them. Whether it was a European booking passage on a boat, a slave chained to a ship, a wagon covered with sailcloth, they all headed toward the unknown with all nonessentials stripped away.

A pioneer has only two things: a deep desire to survive and an equally strong will to live. Home is not the place where our possessions and accomplishments are deposited and displayed. It is this earth that we have explored, the heavens we view with awe, these humans who, despite the flaws, we try to love and those who try to love us. It is the willingness to pioneer the one trek we all can make . . . no matter what our station or location in life . . . the existential reality that wherever there is life . . . we are at home.

BEVERLY BRANCH